# TELLING STORIES ABOUT SCHOOL

## *AN INVITATION. . . .*

**Peter W. Waldron**

**Tani R. Collie**

**Calvin M. W. Davies**

**Merrill,**
an imprint of Prentice Hall

*Upper Saddle River, New Jersey*     *Columbus, Ohio*

**Library of Congress Cataloging-in-Publication Data**

Waldron, Peter W.

    Telling stories about school : an invitation / Peter W. Waldron, Tani R. Collie, Calvin M. W. Davies

    p.   cm.

    Includes bibliographical references and index.

    ISBN 0-13-272386-7

    1. Teachers—Case studies. 2. Teachers—Problems, exercises, etc. 3. Education—Case studies. 4. Education—Problems, exercises, etc. 5. Storytelling.   I. Collie, Tani R. II. Davies, Calvin M. W. III. Title.

LB1775.W185   1999

371.1'0092—dc21                                 97-45708

                                                         CIP

Cover photo: Image Bank
Editor: Debra A. Stollenwerk
Production Editor: Mary M. Irvin
Design Coordinator: Karrie M. Converse
Text Designer: Mia Saunders
Cover Designer: Ceri Fitzgerald
Production Manager: Pamela D. Bennett
Electronic Text Management: Marilyn Wilson Phelps, David Snyder, Karen L. Bretz,
    Tracey B. Ward
Director of Marketing: Kevin Flanagan
Advertising/Marketing Coordinator: Krista Groshong
Marketing Manager: Suzanne Stanton

This book was set in Century Schoolbook by Prentice-Hall, Inc., and was printed and bound by R. R. Donnelley & Sons Company. The cover was printed by Phoenix Color Corp.

© 1999 by Prentice-Hall, Inc.
Simon & Schuster/A Viacom Company
Upper Saddle River, New Jersey 07458

Printed in the United States of America

10 9 8 7 6 5 4 3 2 1

ISBN: 0-13-272386-7

Prentice-Hall International (UK) Limited, *London*
Prentice-Hall of Australia Pty. Limited, *Sydney*
Prentice-Hall of Canada, Inc., *Toronto*
Prentice-Hall Hispanoamericana, S. A., *Mexico*
Prentice-Hall of India Private Limited, *New Delhi*
Prentice-Hall of Japan, Inc., *Tokyo*
Simon & Schuster Asia Pte. Ltd., *Singapore*
Editora Prentice-Hall do Brasil, Ltda., *Rio de Janeiro*

# PREFACE

This book presents personal stories around which are woven reflections, meaning, and insights about schooling. The reflections begin with talk about the beliefs, values, and issues illuminated in the stories. This book is about how the learnings from the stories could be enacted in our lives as teachers. Woven into the fabric of our conversation is the work of other writers, whose ideas provide unique and insightful perspectives that deepen our understanding of the stories. Our search for meaning, through storying and reflection, does not end in solutions or in definitive plans. It is this search we collaboratively embarked on to write and talk about the experiences, ideas, and questions that we value.

Stories are a powerful means of providing images through which readers are able to make personal connections with lived experiences. This book demonstrates how we have learned through the sharing of personal stories and invites readers to reflect on the beliefs and assumptions that influence their work. Current knowledge, coupled with the images emerging from the stories, becomes a basis for uncovering meaning and understanding that drives practice. This critical inquiry into learning, teaching, and organizational thought invites the reader to consider creating the conditions necessary to move from thought to action.

In this book we are trying to model a process for self-reflection that allows for personal connections between day-to-day practice and our contemporary knowledge base. This is not a primary textbook. If it claims textbook status at all it would be in the supplementary mode. The invitational style does not attempt to provide answers. Rather, readers are *invited* to reflect on stories that flow from schooling and to consider subsequent discussion from an often-diverse reference base, in the context of their own beliefs about learning and teaching. For example, the seemingly disparate works of Clandinin, Freire, and Fullan present a challenge for school-based professionals. How do teachers understand the work of these people and glean from their credible and powerful messages, meaning, and understanding for working with young people?

The constant challenge for schools is to gain understanding from our knowledge base in ways that respect the varied contributions of respected scholars and researchers.

The book does not attempt to provide substantial discussion about any one facet of schooling, but invites the reader to consider broad-based references through a personalized response to questions. References cited are supplemented by suggested readings for the reader to pursue, to expand personal meaning and understanding.

Questions that invite thought and talk are important parts of the discussion. The questions we pose are discussed and explored, but not answered. Instead, we invite readers to join us in our reflections as we pose personal questions and share stories of experiences as teachers.

Each chapter is framed by a fundamental question. As the chapter develops, essential questions are posed that invite readers to reflect on and contemplate their beliefs, understandings, and experience. A visual representation of questions is offered at the end of each chapter which may be useful for some readers. These representations, which connect the chapters' essential questions to the fundamental question, may be helpful in illustrating the framework of the chapter. It is this question-posing process that contributes meaning and understanding to ideas within questions, not simple answers.

The book is intended for those who are genuinely interested in the learning that takes place in our schools. We believe the inviting style and tone of the book makes it readable and useful. Pre-service teachers preparing to enter the teaching profession should be able to make connections between the stories and their own knowledge and experience, which should ultimately enhance their view of learning and teaching. The stories could be used to stimulate discussion about life in schools. The subsequent text and questions posed throughout each chapter should inform the discussion from a contemporary knowledge base. Teachers and administrators may find the discussion of current knowledge, through a narrative approach, to be of value in their work with young people. The book could be used for both individual and small group professional development activities.

For those working in teacher education, there are courses at the undergraduate and graduate level for which this is a useful text. The book would clearly connect to courses such as: *Philosophical Study of Educational Theories, Ethics of Teaching, Education and the Social System,* and *Education and the*

*Future.* Our discussion of teaching and learning could make valuable contributions to classes such as: *Education and Individual Development, Learning Theory, Classroom Management, Effective Teacher-Student Interaction, Human Development,* and *Learning and Teaching Strategies.* Classes that focus on curriculum—*Curriculum Foundations, Curriculum Inquiry, Curriculum Change, Curriculum Development*—would all find the book a useful resource to build meaning and understanding. *Administrative Theory, Administrative Leadership, Approaches to Moral Education, Staff Development,* and *Administration and the Role of the Teacher* are courses that focus on leadership in schools toward which this book could make a valuable contribution.

We have found this time of collaboration, storying, and reflection profoundly enriching and rewarding. We hope this book not only tells about some of our experiences, but also creates a space for and values the reader's experiences and reflections. It is our hope that, as schools become more thoughtful places, young people will ultimately benefit.

## ACKNOWLEDGMENTS

We would like to thank the following people for their insightful comments: JoAnne Buggey, University of Minnesota; Ardra L. Cole, Ontario Institute for Studies in Education/University of Toronto; Noble R. Corey, Indiana State University; Susan Dauer, Western Oregon State College; Mary Lynn Hamilton, University of Kansas; James G. Henderson, Kent State University; Valerie J. Janesick, Florida International University; J. Gary Knowles, Ontario Institute for Studies in Education/University of Toronto; Marcella L. Kysilka, University of Central Florida; and Evelyn J. Sowell, Arizona State University, West.

Our sincere thanks to Debra Stollenwerk and Mary Irvin, editors at Prentice Hall, who offered great patience and valuable advice to fledgling authors. Debra Stollenwerk was a pillar of support during the writing and review process. Her convivial manner and gentle suggestions were educational and very helpful. We are similarly grateful to Mary Irvin for her guidance during the production process. Her timely phone calls and openness to our suggestions were appreciated. Thank you also to our copy editor, Key Metts. Her meticulous attention to the manuscript was such that it did not take us long to realize that she was correct!

Peter Waldron                               Calgary, Alberta
Tani Collie                                 December 1997
Calvin Davies

# FOREWORD

## *IMAGINING POSSIBILITIES FOR SCHOOL CHANGE*

This is a book of wonderful stories in which we learn of life in schools. In the preface, we meet the teachers/authors as they begin to tell their stories of working in schools. Their stories are the rich basis for this exploration of life in schools.

Teachers, students, parents, administrators, and researchers are also characters we meet in the pages of the book. We meet Carl, a student whose story makes us stop and ask questions about what stories he lives and tells in his life in school. Carl's story is woven throughout the text and it is through Carl's story that questions about schooling and society are raised. When we turn our attention, as we must, to questions of our own students' lives, this book asks us to consider first what kind of spaces we create for students like Carl. The book then asks us to consider what kind of spaces we create for all of our students in our schools.

As I read the story of parent-teacher interviews, I squirmed as Mr. Green, the teacher, could not recall Bob Wood, one of his students. I wanted to be angry with Mr. Green. But I knew that he was living out an all-too-familiar story of school in which timetables, cycles, and too many students make it difficult to attend with the necessary care to each life being lived out in school.

We read accounts of staff meetings, of professional days, and of opening new schools. We read accounts of subject matter, of evaluation, and of discipline. But the accounts, told as stories, always pushed at the edges, always raised the hard questions. Questions which asked us to consider what stories of school frame our school landscapes? What stories of students are lived and told? What stories of teachers are lived and told?

The book challenges all of us who work in schools to ask questions about our work, to create counter-stories of resistance to the taken-for-granted stories of schools, of students, of teachers. And the book does something remarkable, for it gives all of us imaginative ways to compose these new stories—restorying classroom structures into learning communities, restorying administrative retreats so real questions with hopeful possibilities for changed practices occur, restorying teacher-student dialogue so relationships of mutuality occur, and restorying ourselves through learning to tell and to attend closely to our own stories.

As I read this book, I was also reading Maxine Greene's (1995) book "Releasing the Imagination." Greene writes that she hopes to connect her "own seeking with the strivings of other teachers and teacher educators who are weary of being clerks or technocrats" (p. 2). The authors of this book are ones who will connect with Greene, for they are teachers who are weary of being asked to be clerks. They demand we hear their stories of changing schools. They know well the difficulties of changing schools. Their stories resonate because they are authentic. They show us, again and again, the hopeful possibilities for changing schools so that those of us, students, teachers, administrators, and parents, are enabled to live new stories of community. These stories of possibility resonate, for they are told by people who have worked to shape their schools along more hopeful imaginative plotlines.

D. Jean Clandinin
Centre for Research for Teacher Education and Development
University of Alberta

# ABOUT THE AUTHORS

**PETER WALDRON** is an advocate for public education. He is a practicing principal who believes strongly in principles of democracy within a school community. In his daily work with students, teachers, and parents, he values voice and seeks to create conditions that nurture empowerment, responsibility, and ownership. Within these conditions, collaboration is a way of working, through which he implements understandings of leadership, learning, and school growth and development as they apply to the reality and complexity of life in school.

Peter has taught in Montreal, Calgary, and London, England. He has served as a principal in elementary and secondary schools. At the district level, he has worked as a curriculum consultant, projects coordinator, and director of instructional services.

**TANI COLLIE**'s most recent work has been within an inner-city type of environment of largely lower socio-economic, multicultural families. Her students learned within *learning communities* in which interdisciplinary curriculum, integration of special-needs students, student leadership, and team teaching were typical. Through these experiences, she learned to value the role of voice and choice in her work with students. Integrative curriculum concepts were embraced within innovative models for curriculum implementation. Her leadership role within the learning community concept enabled her to actively implement understandings of narrative inquiry, the subject of her post-graduate work.

**CALVIN DAVIES** is a practicing assistant principal. In his current work with students and teachers, he is searching for ways to effect change in conventional schooling practices. Power and control is, for him, an issue. How do we devolve power and control toward the sharing of responsibility, leadership, and greater feelings of ownership? In his daily work with young people, Calvin listens to their stories and actively seeks their views. He believes strongly in voice and choice for students as they more clearly understand responsibility, accountability, and ownership. Calvin is committed to change in schooling.

# CONTENTS

≋ **CHAPTER 2**

# RESPONDING TO CHANGE 25

≋ **CHAPTER 3**

# HUMANNESS OF THE LEARNER 47

# 1

# THE NEED FOR CHANGE

*AN INVITATION . . .*

In this chapter we invite you to consider the difficult challenges young people face as they try to make meaning of their lives and gain a sense of identity. They live in a complex and rapidly changing society where social, political, and economic institutions adhere to entrenched conventional behaviors. The conventional institutional behaviors of schooling, marked by regularized routines and hierarchical power relationships, inhibit the adaptive capabilities of schools and young people.

**In what ways are schools responding to societal change?**

We believe the way to begin is with self-critical analysis of the deeply held beliefs and values that drive our collective response to young people and their learning. Through reflection, collaboration, and storytelling, schools could deepen their meaning and understanding about learning and teaching. The context of talk, which values voice and promotes mutual trust and respect, brings to the surface personal feelings and beliefs, which help anticipate the future of schools.

❧　❧　❧

❧ IT WAS MY SECOND YEAR of teaching in a high-needs school in southeast Calgary. I thought that this year I would become more used to the dysfunctional homes that most of my students lived in. Alcohol and substance abuse, physical and sexual abuse, poverty, and unemployment were rampant in this multicultural neighborhood. I never thought I would bring one of my students home with me to escape the real-life nightmare that was part of everyday life—until I met Carl. Here is Carl's story.

Carl was basically a good kid. He got into a little trouble, but was able to hold it together for the most part. Lately, I had noticed that Carl's behavior had taken a severe turn for the worse. I seemed to be constantly nagging him about completing his math homework and paying attention to the lesson.

One day Carl got to school at 7:15 a.m. and came down to the room. I was surprised to see him and noticed that he looked extremely exhausted and disheveled. He started talking as soon as he walked in. A real-life horror story poured from his mouth. He described to me in intimate detail the physical abuse he had been subjected to from his father. Things had escalated the previous night to his father throwing plates at him. Carl was covered in bruises and had a severe cut above his left eye. He had spent the night in a shelter. Carl said he had had enough and could not live under these conditions anymore. Together, we went to talk to the school guidance counselor. We called Child Welfare and began to provide Carl with counseling and support.

When I left the counseling office I found myself consumed with Carl's terrible life. I began to wonder how many other students experience family or personal trauma without me or any other teacher realizing it? I began to question the way I had been reacting to Carl during the past few weeks. I had been after him constantly about completing his work. I was concerned that he was falling behind, but I never stopped to find out why he was not doing his work. I had become a teacher of subjects instead of a teacher of students!

Is Carl's situation unusual? Our conversations about the story reminded us of the emotional ties all of us have had with our students. Recollections of those who have had trouble coping with difficult learning and social problems were many and varied. We began to consider the nature of families in today's society and their effects on our students. The view held by Bateson (1990), that "family life provides the metaphors with which we think about the broader ethical relations," (p. 114) provided strong affirmation for our views about the effect of family life on students.

## RAPIDITY AND COMPLEXITY OF SOCIETAL CHANGE

The complexion of family life has altered significantly during the past few decades, and we now see many types of families: nuclear families, single parents, stepparents, foster homes, extended families, and, most recently, families headed by homosexual couples. Although it does not follow that an altered family complexion is necessarily negative, there appears to be increased exposure to stress and vulnerability. Unemployment, intolerance, and violence, among other societal problems, are felt by all families. How are our students and their families adapting to and coping with the pressures of changes in society?

Obviously, Carl could no longer cope with his family. Are young people today developing adequate metaphors for ethics and relationships in their lives? Will students like Carl be able to meet the requirements of the work place, the commitments of relationships with family and friends, and the responsibilities of participation in a democratic society? Carl's story simply reaffirms the often stressful conditions of early adolescence. In these rapidly changing times, young people feel tremendous internal and external pressure and yet many lack the guidance required from family and close adult role models. Freed from the dependency of childhood, they are unable to find the path to adulthood. **How successful are we, in schools, at matching the intellectual, emotional, and interpersonal needs of young people with our educational practices?** As we seek to understand the stresses that are part of our students' lives, we must seriously consider the extent to which learning encourages them to understand and adapt to familial and societal changes.

As we continued our discussions and readings of educational literature, we were increasingly drawn to the realization that, for many students, school adds to the emotional stresses of home. We wonder how much extra stress the initially subject-oriented teacher added to Carl's life? Struggling students are continually confronted with failure, which can harm their sense of self-worth. When we stopped to think about what many of our students face daily at home, we began to see more clearly why in-school learning is particularly difficult for many. **To what extent does in-school learning help students cope with the world around them?** We believe that moral lessons about resolving conflict, working cooperatively and courteously with others, understanding honesty, responsibility, and friendship, and asking oneself, "What is the right thing to do?" are at the heart of successful learning and teaching.

The matter of societal change began to emerge as particularly germane to our conversations about families and schooling. Clearly, the structure of modern society has become more complex, discontinuous (Bateson, 1990), and demanding. Examples of recent changes to our society flowed easily into our conversation. There is a notable multicultural texture, brought about through solicited immigration and refugees uprooted by wars and politics in their homelands. Gender roles are debated and ever-changing, testing the adaptive abilities of both sexes. Increased violence in our country and schools poses frightening concerns and questions. The poverty experienced by many people, some of whom are without homes, provides sad evidence of a changed society and economy. Controversial issues such as homosexuality, abortion, sexually transmitted diseases, and drug abuse—rarely discussed in the past—are now publicly and vehemently debated. The emergence of international trading blocks and a global marketplace has interwoven our economy with the economies of other nations. Pressure to compete with Japan and other economic powers hangs heavily over businesses and corporations. Hostile takeovers, leveraged buy-outs and massive restructuring has been the response, leaving millions unemployed.

Families living in a society marked by this disequilibrium and change cannot help but be affected. Young people find the normal challenge of growing up exacerbated to say the least. Schools face the added difficulties of dealing with the ambiguous demands of a complex society, uncertain expectations of stressful families, and young people struggling to cope. There is little doubt that Carl had been struggling for some time. Is it possible that an altered school structure would have allowed Carl to share his difficulties earlier? The school provided academic learning, but could Carl have been provided with strategies to deal with his home difficulties?

From this rather dismaying glimpse into the life of Carl and that of contemporary society our attention moved to schooling. **What role should schooling play in a society of increasing change and complexity?** What should be considered "basics", so that our young people become competent, contributing, contented members of society? Should we remain faithful to the "three Rs" of traditional schooling? Would a focus on the basics of the past prepare our students for a complicated, discontinuous, contemporary world? As we searched for a definition for *the basics,* we believed it was important to understand learning in the broadest sense. Social learning is just as important as academic learning. Our young people desperately require help in understanding such societal concerns as violence, family breakdown, poverty, multiculturalism, and gender issues, along with other moral and ethical considerations.

The onset of the Information Age and the massive role of technology in our world, we believe, extends the traditional academic basics to include a focus on problem posing and solving, critical thinking, understanding and use of technology, reflection, and metacognition. The business world cries out for employees who are able to collaborate, communicate, and think creatively. **To what extent should the needs of contemporary society become part of the basics for schooling?**

WHEN I WAS IN SCHOOL I was what teachers called a good student. I completed my work, achieved honors grades, and was respectful of my classmates and teachers. For the most part, I liked my teachers and they liked me. Memories of school, from my adult perspective, are basically positive. One incident, though, always flashes into focus as I reflect on my schooling.

I sat beside John McGregor in Mrs. Smith's social studies class. John was frequently verbally and physically abused by his father. Always having been drawn to those who need support or help, I had developed a friendship with John. One day John had come to social studies class without a pen or pencil. As usual, Mrs. Smith began the lesson with a lecture and notes on the overhead for us to copy. I knew John would get into trouble if he came to class without something to write with, so I slowly unzipped my overstuffed pencil case and handed it to John, whispering, "John, here's a pencil."

Mrs. Smith, red-faced in anger, yelled, "Tracy and John get out of my classroom and march directly down to the office". I, of course, had never been sent to the office, but I had heard that it wasn't a great place to be "sent". On my way out, I tried to plead my case, but she wouldn't listen to me. I begged her not to send John, because I was the one who interrupted. She would hear none of it. We walked slowly to the office, each immersed in our own thoughts and feelings. My mind was spinning. I lamented over how disappointed my parents would be when they got the phone call from the office! I feared the reaction of John's father, and I was angry and hurt at the unjust treatment we had received from Mrs. Smith.

I sat quietly in the principal's office as he spoke about being disruptive in class. It quickly became obvious to me that he had already heard from Mrs. Smith and would be unsympathetic to my side of the story.

Shortly thereafter I was told that my parents would receive a phone call about the incident and I was to go home and talk to them about it. As I left the office, I heard the principal call John in. I assume he called John's parents also, because he was not at school for the rest of the week. Unfortunately, I didn't need to ask why.

For a young girl who consistently worked hard and genuinely liked school, the experience with Mrs. Smith left Tracy with feelings of bitterness and disillusionment. Tracy had thought Mrs. Smith had reciprocated her respect, but clearly she had mistaken respect for appreciation of her quiet passive behavior. Her voice was also silenced by the principal. How often do we silence the voices of young people in our schools? Doesn't it seem strange that students most often have the quietest and weakest voices in buildings which are intended for them? Do we respect and adapt to the unique needs and talents of individual students? John definitely had particular needs which were neither respected nor cared for. **How do hierarchical relationships and structures in schools affect young people and their learning?** The power structure became obvious in the story when Mrs. Smith sent Tracy and John out of *her* class to the office. She had power over the students, and the principal had power over all. We believe the questions and concerns which emanated from the story are ones that are applicable to schools throughout time. Why, we wondered, does schooling continue to be so resistant to change? We discussed four factors:

- conventional institutional behavior of schooling
- hierarchical organizational relationships
- tradition and schooling
- power and control

## Conventional Institutional Behavior of Schooling

To help us gain a deeper understanding about the hierarchical, "power over" ways that schools use in responding to young people, our conversation moved to the nature of schooling as an institution. How do institutions respond to change? They are driven by organizational behaviors and bureaucracies that tend to be driven heavily by routine and convention. Examples of deeply entrenched traditions in institutions easily made their way into our conversation. The precedent-driven legal system's mystique is perpetuated by traditional apparel and archaic language. The practice of religion takes cues from scriptures written centuries ago. Medicine adheres to scientific-diagnostic-prescriptive approaches to illness with often arrogant disregard for established practices from other cultures.

These traditions embedded and upheld in law, religion, and medicine have proved resistant to change. The same is true of education. We all have stories about attempts at making major or minor changes in a school. The common thread running through all of them is the skepticism, cynicism, defensiveness, or downright rejection we faced when the change was suggested. The fact that schooling has its own time-honored institutional behaviors became clear to us.

In fact, Tracy and John's story demonstrates an example of traditional behavior in handling discipline concerns with young people. Do these resilient, enduring traditions best serve students entering the twenty-first century?

We believe the schooling traditions of the past do not meet the needs of today's students. The Information Age, with all its technology-inspired upheavals, has imposed itself with overwhelming speed, and societal institutions, including schools, are experiencing difficulty adapting to changing conditions. We posed a question that proved to be uncomfortable, difficult, and frustrating. **What conditions could result from the rapid pace of social change and the difficulty of institutions to adapt to that change?**

## Hierarchical Organizational Relationships

To be viable and effective, institutions have an intrinsic need to maintain control. Tracy and John's school is a telling example of this. The maintenance of control, consistent routines, and a clear power structure were perceived to be necessary to an effective school. Imagine an attempt to restructure this school. The tension between the need to change and the need to maintain control would likely be manageable if the forces of change were slow. However, if the change were rapid, Mrs. Smith and most others would have responded with anxiety and defensiveness. Bolman and Deal (1991) refer to social control as being essential to those in institutions who are in formal positions; only if the system remains viable do they retain authority. Their positions can be undermined if partisan conflict becomes too powerful to control. Further difficulties arise with the involvement and demands of different constituent groups. The task of hearing and honoring the voices of all stakeholders involved in a schooling endeavor becomes more complicated. When change is slow, orchestrating constituent involvement is manageable. But power management is more complex, especially in today's tenuous times. We were strongly influenced by the writing of Sarason (1990) on the extreme complexity of trying to change power relationships in institutions insulated by years of tradition.

Our conversation ended with more questions than answers. How could a school like the one Tracy and John attended change to better honor the needs of its young people? What approach could we take to the problem posed by rapid societal change and the resistance to change inherent in institutions?

꩜ I WAS HALFWAY THROUGH MY SECOND EVENING of parent-teacher interviews. My head was spinning with information. Which student was I going to give extra help to? Who would be placed on a day book? Who needs some enrichment? Whom was I going to call in a week? Talk about information overload. . . . I was fried! Just when I thought I might have a moment to collect my thoughts, a parent rushed up to my table. "Hello, hello Mr. Allison," she said enthusiastically. "I have been looking forward to meeting you for weeks. I am Mrs. Wood, Bob's mom."

I greeted Mrs. Wood politely and invited her to be seated. My eyes darted around the gymnasium hoping to catch a glimpse of Bob making his way toward me. No such luck, I would have to bide my time with chit chat as I racked my brain for a connection. Bob, I thought, this is not a good year for the name Bob. I teach seven Bobs out of a possible 210 students. "Oh, Mr. Allison, Bob really likes science, he says you are his favorite teacher."

"Well, Bob is a really nice kid and I am happy to hear that he likes science. It is a real hands-on type of class." I felt as though I was turning red. My mind was racing trying to figure out which Bob it was. I was sure I did not teach a Bob Wood and I thought she must be his stepmother. I could not take it any longer, so I just asked, "Which grade is Bob in?" Mrs. Wood seemed puzzled that I did not know but, nonetheless, she told me that her son was in my seventh-grade science class. That narrowed it down to one of three possible classes, so I opened my mark book and scanned the classes. Sure enough, in 7E, there was Bob Wood. All assignments had been turned in and his mark was 62%. Now I could talk to his mom about how well I knew her son and what we could do together to improve and enhance the possibilities for Bob's achievement, success, and good feelings. Yeah, right!

---

How many teachers face the frustration of teaching a large number of students, but only getting to know and understand a few? Why is it that many schools cycle large numbers of students through many teachers? Is this practice based on the needs and interests of students?

## Tradition and Schooling

As we explored these questions it became clear that many of our organizational practices and routines are based on a model for schooling with roots in decades past. The more we talked about traditional school routines and practices, the more we understood how they have become "regularized" (Sarason, 1972). When public education first became available to vast numbers of young people during the last century, industrial management practices in vogue at the time were employed to manage children and their learning. The "factory model" for schooling became established during the Industrial Revolution, at which time production methods of specialization and departmentalization were used.

We could not help but wonder to what degree things have really changed. In these early days of public schooling, students were placed on a "conveyor belt." Each classroom became a "filling station" of knowledge. Classroom work and activities were neatly compartmentalized by subject areas in this fragmented approach to schooling. Students saw little connection between the "stops" as they continued their assembly-line journey. We talked about the schools in which we have worked during the past ten years and contemplated the significance of the changes since the beginnings of public schooling in the last century. Clearly there have been many changes, but have they been significant? In our story, Mr. Allison was the science specialist, his classroom was part of the science department and students flowed through like products on an assembly line.

Our profession has experienced an incredible increase in knowledge in recent years, bringing us new insights and understandings about the nature of young people and how they learn. We have spent many hours in schools working with these insights with teachers and young people. It is simply not easy working with students in new ways. We believe school-based people have particular complexities in this regard. Like professionals in any field, teachers have a responsibility to be aware of current knowledge, to sort through its implications and make sense out of it for their work with young people. They must do this in the context of the incredible busyness that characterizes life in school. A real tendency exists to pursue particular trends and innovations, and this has contributed to a "flavor-of-the-month" accusation: the amorphous drifting from one trend to another without incorporating the merits of any into a personal belief system. It's probably easier to fall back on the tried-and-true and the familiar! Not only do the institutional conventions make things difficult, but the patterning and experiences of students, teachers, and parents also present hurdles. Imagine how difficult would it be for those in Mr. Allison's school to change the focus on specialization and departmentalization, when teachers and students have worked that way for so long.

In the early twentieth century, technical–scientific thought characterized especially by the work of Taylor (1911), enriched the cruder methods of the previous century, leaving indelible impressions on the practice of and design for learning in schooling. Teaching that demanded rational, objective approaches to curriculum design and measurement denied the individuality of young people. Linear, scientific approaches to learning assumed that groups of students should learn at the same rate and in the same way. These conventions and routines seem to have become entrenched to the point where they epitomize the regularization of which Sarason (1972) speaks. The plight of Bob's teacher in our story is symptomatic of regularized procedures and their insensitivity to the real needs of students, parents, and teachers. As we talked about this insensitivity, we realized that educators have departed only sporadically from this regularized course since the beginning of the twentieth century. Even the wisdom and insight of John Dewey did not affect the regularized routines of schooling practice in any enduring and pervasive sense. Such is the power of the institution. As a result, the traditional model is still evident in schools.

Our story about Bob's teacher reminds us that schools are not solely buildings, machines, and curriculum. Schools are relationships among people. The former has dominated the institution of schooling; an institution that has been objectively managed and in which a convention-driven bureaucracy resides. **Why is it that schooling has worshipped the regular and persistently avoided significant change?** We are attracted to the conclusion that it is because the glue of social convention in our schools has nurtured social acceptance. The speed of societal change for most of the twentieth century has been such that the relative tradition of schooling is seen almost affectionately as a healthy base of stability.

Unfortunately, changes within society have become endemic. The school, once revered as a haven of tradition, is now a target of societal disaffection. A maelstrom of discontent is brewing among constituents—parents, the business community, politicians, special interest groups, and so on—and interventions to assume power are disturbing. The conventions that permeate the institution of schooling, once a source of strength and stability, are now the millstone that denies the ability to adapt. The frustrations experienced by Bob's teacher were a symptom of the school's lack of adaptive abilities. The teacher deeply felt the frustrations and was compelled to use his intellectual wiles to obscure his ignorance. If we "tell the truth about current reality" (Senge, 1990, p. 54), we might uncover numerous examples similar to that experienced by Bob's teacher. We strongly believe that schools must adopt more adaptive and generative approaches to learning not only to serve young people well, but also to survive.

🙠 *INCIDENT 1:* A STUDENT RAN FROM THE WASHROOM shouting, "Fire! Fire!" The alarm sounded and the school was cleared. Luckily, the fire was contained in a urinal and there were no injuries. On the next day, the bathroom was locked and the principal addressed the student body over the P.A. system. "Due to the fire in the west boy's washroom yesterday, the washroom has been locked until we find out who was involved." A week passed and the washroom was unlocked, even though the culprits were not discovered.

*Incident 2:* The students had just made their way to the fourth period of the morning when the alarm sounded. Binders were closed, chairs pushed in, the lights turned off, and the door was closed. Teachers and students filed down the hallway and out the front door. Attendance was taken and the students were then escorted back into the building. Over the P.A., the principal indicated that it was a false alarm and that the student who caused the disruption to their learning had been caught and was sitting in his office. This student would be charged and fined as per the fire code.

*Incident 3:* The school day had drawn to a close, students and many teachers had cleared the building for the day and made their way home. A few students could be spotted in a wrestling practice, while a few others hung out in the main hallway lingering and talking. The fire alarm sounded, the practice came to a halt and the school was cleared. Flames had erupted from a display board. Were it not for the quick thinking of a caretaker the school would have been ablaze in seconds.

The following morning staff members were greeted by a locked front door. After a couple of knocks the principal swung open the door and informed the staff of an emergency staff meeting scheduled for 8 a.m., in the staff room. As the staff gathered the atmosphere was ablaze with conversation about the previous day's incident. The principal entered the room and outlined what had happened and his decision on what would be done. "We will be closing the halls," he decreed. "Students will not be allowed into the building until 8:15 a.m., they will have 15 minutes to eat their lunches after which they will be ushered outside for the remainder of the noon hour. After school the building will be cleared of all students within 15 minutes of the bell." The principal indicated that he would like to talk to student council representatives during the first period. At that time he would present a memo to the council outlining the closed-hall policy. Council members would then go back to class to give the information to their classmates.

"I don't think we should have the students read the message," bellowed one staff member.

"I'm giving a test first period, I do not want the interruption," exclaimed another.

"We lose enough time as it is, besides, you should deliver the message, Mr. Principal." The consensus of the staff was that the students needed to hear the message from someone in authority.

So, off he went to give his speech: Halls will be closed until we find out who is responsible.

We wonder what the atmosphere was like in the school that morning after the third incident? Staff gossip would be rife. Students would be looking at each other wondering who might be responsible. Teachers would be offering their own opinions about how the principal handled the situation. Was he firm enough? Was he flexible enough? Would the students learn their lesson? What in fact are we doing to ourselves as teachers, and what are we doing to our young people? Three questions beg for answers in the story: What is motivating the administration in its response to the fires? What message is conveyed by the behavior of the staff? What are the students learning from these incidents?

## Power and Control

We consider the school a classic example of a convention-bound place where the power and control vested in authority is used to manage students and their learning. We see students who would likely exhibit a "we–they" attitude toward their teachers, who would probably reflect a similar attitude. In these situations the ones with the greatest power wield their "clubs" to get what they want from the ones with the least power. Schools do this quite often. Behaviors are usually cloaked in the language of pedagogy, providing reasons and explanations that sound professional and wise. We would argue that a change in the understanding of and attitude toward power and control is needed for the voices of students to be included and respected. Revenge has no place in a learning environment. Children who are managed through power and control will learn to use power and control to get their own way. When schools punish all children for the actions of one or two, the frustrations of the ones in power, as a result of "having their noses tweaked," can be described only as revenge.

In our story, the teachers and the principal were the ones with the power. How did they use power and control in the fire situation? We recognize the complexity of school life. We understand that trying to change power relationships (Sarason, 1990) in these complex places is difficult. All this notwithstanding, we are of the firm opinion that schools must shed their power-related conventional behaviors, where children must fit what the adults "know" to be best for them. Schools must become more adaptive and generative in their responses to young people and their learning. Two extremely important elements are missing in the school:

1. responsibility
2. ownership

To what extent are the students responsible for the fire incidents? And who owns the problem? We believe the answers to these questions go beyond the incidents in question. If responsibility and ownership are part of the fabric of learning in the school and young people are allowed and encouraged to assume responsibility for their learning, then what would the school's response have been?

What if the school's young people had been expected to take ownership for their learning and behavior by practicing decision-making skills and experiencing collective response? The fires would immediately become the collaborative concern of the entire school. As it was, the teachers—or more precisely, the principal—owned the problem. Glickman (1990) writes powerfully about ownership in schools. He speaks of people circumscribing problems by assigning responsibility to others, but also, if necessary, to assign blame. Through this kind of action one doesn't have to take any responsibility. We believe that matters of responsibility and ownership are fundamental to schools adapting their understanding of power and control.

---

⌒ As AN ADMINISTRATIVE TEAM we had been meeting together for about two months, trying to prepare for the opening of a new school year. I think we got off to a really good start. We spent the best part of two days sharing our beliefs about teaching and learning. The feeling among us was positively electric. We were going to break down the pillars of tradition and liberate the education system. We talked about student voice, choice, responsibility, authentic assessment, shared decision-making, and an assortment of other terms that stimulate the juices of educators.

During these discussions, I wondered how deep our individual and collective understanding of these terms was? The first test came when we faced the need to finalize our timetable. The initial framework was in place, but there was a problem in the physical education and optional-class area. How many option choices and how much time should be spent in a given area were questions that caused some concern. As the conversation ensued it became clear that we were simply managing learning. We lacked a collective understanding of why we should make a particular decision. It had been two months since we had talked about our beliefs and values and many agenda items had been checked off. There was even a feeling that because we lived our beliefs as a group, there was no need to revisit and deepen our understanding of what each of us believed to be important. We needed to find a balance between the need to get things done and the need to understand why we want to do what we do.

---

This story illustrates that the adaptive and generative potential that schools must pursue is not consistent with the nature of schooling as a traditional institution. The teacher realized that the essence of the matter centered on understanding. We believe that a radical rethinking is required of the ways we:

1. understand and respond to young people
2. understand learning
3. invite young people to build knowledge and make meaning
4. understand the places where our young people learn

## EXAMINING ASSUMPTIONS ABOUT LEARNING

The ability to adapt in pedagogical, administrative, and organizational contexts means seeing beyond the detail of the bigger picture and being ready to adjust the details to suit the larger purposes (Low, 1993a). This is where the school in our story seemed to have difficulties. We were constantly drawn to our understanding of schooling as an institution. The regularized routines and behaviors of a convention-driven institution mark leadership, administrative, and pedagogical practices. These practices cause difficulties in demonstrating and sustaining adaptive abilities. What are schools to do? The secret is deceptively simple: "It is simply a matter of having a deep understanding of the most important things that ought to be done and then making sure that they are done effectively" (Low, 1993b).

This reminder brought us back to the question of understandings. As we pondered the story, we realized that our desire for deeper understanding must be ongoing. It is the continuous inquiry into and reflection on practice in the quest for congruency with contemporary knowledge that will bring this about. Depth of understanding, profoundness of meaning, and the conditions to effect both, constitute an essential focus for effective schooling. How many more questions or issues will the school in our story deal with before its central, agreed-on purpose is solidified within a process that allows for ongoing challenge to add depth and clarity of meaning? If such a process is not developed, the school will inevitably engage in activities because they are required by the administration, suggested by an enthusiastic staff member, demanded by the superintendent, or simply the latest trend. Whatever the reason, they did not emanate from a collective response to the learning needs of young people in the particular school. Low's (1993b) deep understanding of what needs to be done was absent. Understandings were superficial at best. We considered focus, adaptive behavior, and school action, and we think the schema in Figure 1.1 provides a useful framework within which this kind of thinking can occur. We discussed three areas:

- mental models and tacit assumptions
- adaptive behavior
- voice, talk, and collaboration

## Mental Models and Tacit Assumptions

We continued to explore the need for change and our talk centered on the motivations for understandings and actions. Why do we do the things we do in schooling? Why do we organize for learning in the regimented ways of traditional schooling? Do children learn best through grade structures? Is learning

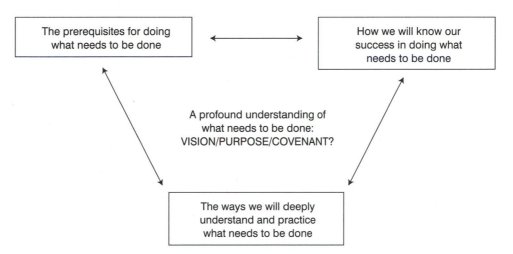

The prerequisites for doing
what needs to be done

How we will know our
success in doing what
needs to be done

A profound understanding of
what needs to be done:
VISION/PURPOSE/COVENANT?

The ways we will deeply
understand and practice
what needs to be done

**FIGURE 1.1**   Adaptive Behaviors in Schools

as predictable as our actions suggest? When we plan a five-week unit and test students at the end, are we not assuming that all our students should have learned what we have taught them? How can we do this and at the same time declare that all children are unique, learning in different ways and at different rates? Our motivations are driven by unexamined assumptions about children and their learning.

Senge (1990) presented a message we found compelling. He speaks of *mental models:* inner patterns of thought that drive and, indeed, govern our behavior. Mental models essentially determine how we present ourselves to the world; our thoughts and actions. But what really seemed powerful to us was Senge's caution that mental models are often tacit—we are not aware of their presence. We realized how troublesome this tacitness is in schooling. If mental models are the ways we understand and respond to our world and are often tacit, then schooling behaviors that need to change become problematic. Any tacitly held behavior-driving mental models are not available for challenge. They will continue to inspire and influence attitudes, understandings, and behavior toward conventional practice, even while overt intentions may be considering change. We pondered this at some length and it seemed to be almost a latent paradox that contributes significantly to the institutional lethargy that marks the reluctance of schooling to respond vigorously to change.

Our reading then brought us to Newman (1987) and her work on assumptions. Newman speaks of tacit forces that drive our beliefs about teaching and learning. These assumptions are comparable to the mental models of which Senge speaks. They cause us to operate a good deal of the time "from an intuitive sense of what is going on without actively reflecting on what our intentions might be and what our actions might be saying to students" (Newman

1987, p. 727). As we talked about Newman's ideas we could not help being drawn back to the school story about the fires. Did the school administrators actively reflect on their intentions and what their actions might be saying to the students? We wondered about the depth of the school's understanding of what ought to be done. To what extent was the school's response to the incidents associated with those deeply held beliefs and values about learning that drive the collective response? "Our beliefs about learning and teaching can only be uncovered by engaging in systematic, self-critical analysis of our current instructional practices" (Newman 1987, p. 727). We believe this systematic, ongoing, self-critical analysis is a fundamental aspect of change needed in schooling. Only through this practice will schools uncover and challenge the tacit assumptions and mental models that drive their understandings and attitudes toward young people and their learning.

≋ WHEN I LOOK BACK ON MY FIRST YEAR AS A TEACHER, many thoughts, feelings, and experiences flash into my mind like snapshots in a family album. Like the snapshots, my memories are fragmented representations of the time and bring many feelings back from the past: anticipation and fear, reward and disappointment, loneliness and love, frustration and success. One snapshot in particular brings forth myriad emotional and thought-provoking memories: I was trying to teach fractions. Five minutes or so into the lesson I knew the students weren't grasping the concept at all and I needed to try a new approach. My second method confused and frustrated them even more. By that time they were getting sick of listening to me and were becoming disruptive. Finally I admitted to the class, "I am getting so frustrated I could scream!"

"Well, we're so frustrated we could scream, too," one boy replied.

Without pausing to think, I switched off the lights and began to scream. Soon all the students joined me in this cathartic experience. The teacher from across the hall burst into my classroom (the first time he had ever been in), turned on the lights, and yelled, "Be quiet!" He asked me if I was all right and left as quickly as he came. We sat there in exhausted silence, looking at each other, all of us wondering what was to come next. A student quietly spoke, "Mrs. Lee, can I say something?" This began an honest, critical examination of our class and how it might work more successfully. The students shared how and from whom they liked to learn, and I shared my feelings and thoughts.

The tone, structure, and relationships in class were changed that day when we screamed in mutual frustration. It seems you often have to be on the verge of disaster, face-to-face with failure, or screaming in frustration, before change occurs.

What made this a story of success instead of failure? How did the experience, which began as a struggle, end as a positive one for both the students and the teacher? Perhaps it was the adaptive behavior exhibited by all that made the difference. After the screaming, the conversations focused on how they could adapt to one another to make the classroom a more welcoming, successful place. This brief story is an example of the importance of adaptive behavior for people and institutions in our rapidly changing world.

## Adaptive Behavior

We began to consider adaptive behavior more closely and found the ideas of Rohrkemper and Corno (1988) to be persuasive. They see adaptive learning as a constellation of attitudes and skills that enhance our abilities to act independently. Within a student body, it is the ability of young people who are capable of adapting to and modifying circumstances handed them: students who can respond flexibly and proactively to stressful situations and also initiate tasks that challenge their abilities. These students could assume control of their own learning. Adaptive learning, the self-control that involves confronting and coping with stressful learning by modifying the task or the self, allows students to compensate for many of the realities of the educational system and society. As a teacher, Mrs. Lee exhibited this type of adaptive learning, and by allowing her students to have a voice, she encouraged them to display adaptive learning as well.

It is not sufficient to talk of students being adaptive in their learning. Schooling, as an institution, must demonstrate adaptive abilities. As we reflected on Newman's (1987) comments about assumptions and the problems of their tacitness, it became clear to us that the honest challenging of the assumptions that drive the practices of schooling is not only important but also central to adaptive capability. Our work together in writing this book was in fact modeling the advice of Newman, when she speaks about the need to engage in "systematic, self-critical analysis." The conditions that describe the day-to-day work in schools must encourage staffs to engage in analysis of the understandings of learning, teaching, and organizational thought that drive their work with young people.

We believe the dynamics of life in schools are not fully appreciated by many who do not live this life. Anybody whose work is associated with schooling tends to have an agenda for schools. Schools, therefore, represent the confluence for these agendas. It is paradoxical, if not ironic, that those in schools who must interpret, understand, and discriminatingly implement the agendas are those who possess neither the luxury of time to do so nor the support that transcends the patronizingly moral. This is a fundamental point which urgently needs to be addressed by in-district and out-of-district professionals.

Bateson (1990) speaks of creative improvisation as a model for adaptive behaviors in response to a changing world. Creative improvisation seems to describe accurately Mrs. Lee's actions in the story. For Mrs. Lee, "on the verge of disaster," creative improvisation became a tool for survival. Perhaps schools need to become places of creative improvisation and more adaptive, to meet the needs of our young people. We discussed traditional responses to learning by schools. Grade levels, units of study, unit tests, streaming, whole-class teaching, management of curriculum, management of time, management of people—the list seems endless. Do our responses emanate from an understanding of student learning needs? Or do they generally emanate from judgments that adults make about what is best for young people? We concur with Bateson (1990) that schools must learn to "adjust to discontinuity" and that this is the emerging problem of our era. We see creative improvisation as synonymous with adaptation. But if schools are to become creative improvisers and adaptive to change, what would such places look like?

## Voice, Talk, and Collaboration

What is the teacher's role in creating a school focused on adaptation and improvisation? Clandinin (1993), in her discussion of voice, emphasizes the importance of teachers sharing their stories. We realized that in the conventional, regularized environments of many schools, the stories of teachers have not been honored and the knowledge that teachers hold has not been shared. Even before we met, the connections between us had begun to form. Our experiences as teachers had lead us to interwoven questions and stories about teaching, schools, and students. We shared the intention of making classrooms more caring, creative, and dynamic places. Our stories contained frustration and concern for the seeming lack of dignity and honor with which our young people were treated in schools. When we finally met, these connected experiences and stories brought us together. Our work began with genuine talk about schools, our lives, and our visions for the future. In our voices we heard deeply held beliefs about education, teaching and learning. It is through talk that our beliefs and assumptions are self-critically analyzed:

> "Talk" is essential. It is through talk that teachers [students] and administrators articulate their beliefs and values and expectations, their understandings of the context and their uncertainties, and that they come to know the beliefs and values and expectations, the understandings and uncertainties of others. (LaRoque & Downie, 1993, p. 1)

"Talk," sharing our stories and creating places for our voices to be heard became important, valued experiences. We shared our stories in the early mornings by our mail boxes, during moments in the hallway during class changes, and in brief encounters in the office, the staff room, and the library. Together, the three of us found spaces to collaborate, where the genuine and valued stories we shared helped us understand and make meaning of our lives as teachers. Soon, chance meetings in the middle of busy school days became inadequate and we began to meet in our strangely quiet classrooms early in the morning or after school and in the living rooms or patios of our homes. Our conversations were filled with stories about our daily work with young people and reflections on the meaning and understandings embedded in our experiences. The theme of our talk always revolved around the question: How do we make schools better places for students to learn?

Of course, we never had the answer, or a recipe for concocting the most effective school, but we discovered our meetings were effecting changes—changes in the ways we knew and talked about ourselves as teachers and changes in our daily work with young people. As these changes occurred we realized the power and importance of collaboration and reflection in teaching life. What had begun as unplanned, pleasurable conversations, had evolved into necessary relationships that supported, challenged, and enhanced each of us and our work in schools. The relationship we shared allowed us to voice our personal beliefs about learning and teaching, pose questions about current educational practice and issues, and risk making changes within ourselves and our classrooms. The more we talked and listened to one another the more we came to understand ourselves and make meaning of our work. It is this search for meaning and understanding, using collaboration and reflection as our guide, that we share in this book. Collaboration, often perceived as simply a feel-good activity with little meaning or direction, is in fact important to the learning and teaching culture in schools.

Our collaborative relationship enabled the telling of stories, meaningful conversations, and anticipation of the future of schooling. It was an empowering, professional, and motivating beginning. In the previous story, how might Mrs. Lee have benefited from a collaborative relationship with her more experienced colleague across the hall? Do these relationships exist in schools today? **To what extent do young people benefit from learning environments that deepen understandings toward creative improvisation and adaptation?** Regrettably the traditional approaches to schooling—the regularized strategies of our technical–rational institution—continue to dominate and, harsh as it may sound, deny many young people the satisfaction of success.

〜 CHRIS WAS A WONDERFUL, SOCIABLE PERSON. He was at ease with people of all ages. It was not unusual for him to drop in to visit a friend and, if the friend were not home, spend many hours visiting with the parents. He was an outgoing young man. On a number of occasions he spoke his piece in formal sessions with adults. Visiting tradesmen have been impressed with his willingness and ability to help. In the ninth grade, he was active and effective in contributing to his school's seventy-fifth anniversary celebrations. And then there was his sense of humor. Ah yes, beware his sense of humor! He was a master of situational comedy. The Hunch Back of Notre Dame, the outrageous statement with a straight face, the aggressive bully, the voices of many characters, especially the menacing organized-crime thug and the village idiot—all were staples of his repertoire. Chris was a warm, convivial and funny person to be with.

But schoolwork was not Chris's forte. His success began to wane once he moved into the secondary grades. Indeed, in the eighth grade, he began to experience notable learning difficulties. In high school, as he sat in the third row, second seat from the back, he was required to listen to his teacher's lecture, ask questions, and place notes on the blackboard for copying into notebooks. Duplicated note sheets and worksheets filled his binders. Seldom was he invited to participate in group discussions, make choices, voice his opinion, or engage in learning that was in any way connected to his life. Chris experienced increasing frustration and generally disliked school. He finally made it through high school, but what about life for Chris after school? He left school feeling no good, I suspect even incompetent. He shied away from learning, unless he really wanted to do it. Engaging in new learning to enrich his life required risk-taking; something he was hesitant to do. He expected he would fail!

Sadly, Chris died at the age of 18 after a debilitating struggle with a brain tumor—a tragic metaphor, perhaps. Had he lived, his debilitating struggle with in-school learning would hardly have launched him into a life of confidence and challenge. But Chris was a vital young man. He would not want his friends bemoaning his struggles. He would want them to get out and party on his behalf! For those of us who knew Chris, or who know young people like him in our schools, let us see in his story a challenge. Let us reflect on what we do with young people in the name of learning, and consider whether we respect them as unique and vital individuals. How might we nurture their inherent abilities and talents toward a successful and vibrant life? How might Chris's struggle lead us toward a changing view of schooling? I am a better person for having known and loved Chris. He was my son. I hope and pray that Chris's struggles in school might inspire us toward ways of learning that truly respect uniqueness and diversity in young people.

## An Invitation to the Reader

The following page suggests a process for thinking about the chapter, to stimulate conversation, encourage debate, share stories, provoke further questions, challenge current thinking, or engage in further personal reflection. University classes, professional development groups, school staffs, and parent groups may find the chapter's questions and related text useful, as a challenge to personal beliefs, understandings and experiences, toward affirmation or change.

We present the concept of "filter." Readers are invited to consider the central question of the chapter, along with the questions that arise from the text. It is not our intention to limit or reduce context to one small portion of the chapter—we are conscious of the problem of reductionism. It is our hope that, as readers proceed through the book, they will respond to questions in a more holistic manner.

The concept of filter is a metaphor for the reader's personal beliefs, values, and experiences, through which new ideas are explored and current beliefs challenged. It is this filtering that provides an opportunity for the reader to make personal connections to the questions and ideas in the chapter. This process may provide an opportunity to deepen meaning and understanding of the concepts and ideas discussed.

**In the following framework, you are invited to contemplate your beliefs, understandings, and experiences through reflecting on the questions and related text in Chapter 1.**

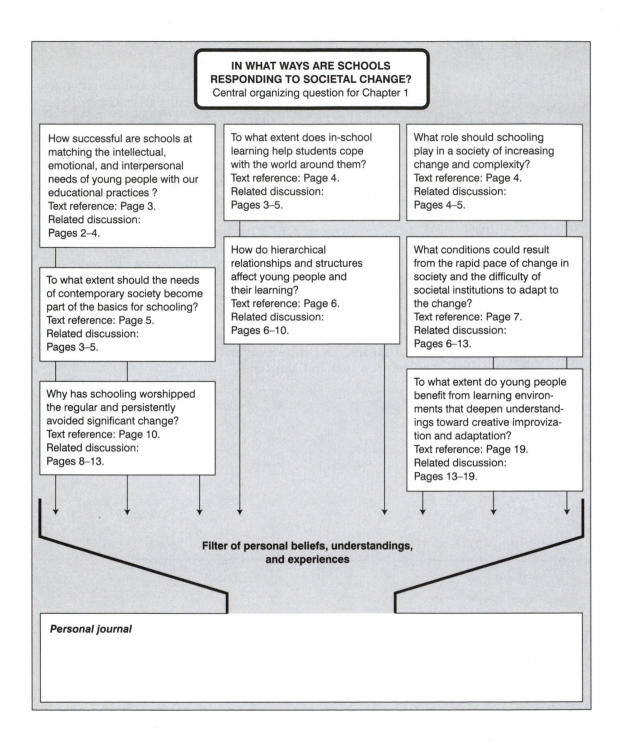

**IN WHAT WAYS ARE SCHOOLS RESPONDING TO SOCIETAL CHANGE?**
Central organizing question for Chapter 1

How successful are schools at matching the intellectual, emotional, and interpersonal needs of young people with our educational practices ?
Text reference: Page 3.
Related discussion:
Pages 2–4.

To what extent does in-school learning help students cope with the world around them?
Text reference: Page 4.
Related discussion:
Pages 3–5.

What role should schooling play in a society of increasing change and complexity?
Text reference: Page 4.
Related discussion:
Pages 4–5.

To what extent should the needs of contemporary society become part of the basics for schooling?
Text reference: Page 5.
Related discussion:
Pages 3–5.

How do hierarchical relationships and structures affect young people and their learning?
Text reference: Page 6.
Related discussion:
Pages 6–10.

What conditions could result from the rapid pace of change in society and the difficulty of societal institutions to adapt to the change?
Text reference: Page 7.
Related discussion:
Pages 6–13.

Why has schooling worshipped the regular and persistently avoided significant change?
Text reference: Page 10.
Related discussion:
Pages 8–13.

To what extent do young people benefit from learning environments that deepen understandings toward creative improvization and adaptation?
Text reference: Page 19.
Related discussion:
Pages 13–19.

**Filter of personal beliefs, understandings, and experiences**

*Personal journal*

# REFERENCES

Bateson, M. C. (1990). *Composing a life*. New York: Atlantic Monthly Press.

Bolman, L., & Deal, T. (1991). *Reframing organizations*. San Francisco: Jossey-Bass Publishers.

Clandinin, D. J. (1993). *Learning to teach, teaching to learn*. New York: Teachers' College Press.

Glickman, C. (1990). *Renewing America's schools*. San Francisco: Jossey-Bass Publishers.

LaRoque, L., & Downie, R. (1993). Staff collaboration. *Educator's Notebook 4*(4).

Low, K. (1993a). *Educational design for the 21st century*. Unpublished manuscript, Action Studies Institute, Calgary, Alberta.

Low, K. (1993b). *Designing schools for the 21st century—Critical assessment No. 4*. Calgary Board of Education 10th Annual Summer Institute for Administrative Teams, Calgary, Alberta.

Newman, J. (1987). Learning to teach by uncovering our assumptions. *Language Arts, 67*(7).

Rohrkemper, M., & Corno, L. (1988). Success and failure on classroom tasks: Adaptive learning and classroom teaching. *The Elementary School Journal, 88*(3).

Sarason, S. (1972). *The creation of settings and the future societies*. San Francisco: Jossey-Bass.

Sarason, S. (1990). *The predictable failure of educational reform*. San Francisco: Jossey-Bass.

Senge, P. (1990, Fall). The leader's new work: Building learning organizations. *Sloan Management Review*. Boston: Massachusetts Institute of Technology.

Taylor, F. (1911). *The principles of scientific management*. New York: W. W. Norton and Co.

# SUGGESTED READINGS

You may be interested in SERGIOVANNI'S (1995) critiques of the traditional view of schools as formal organizations in his book, *Building Community in Schools,* published by Jossey-Bass (San Francisco). He offers a theory of community as an alternative to the traditional view. His theory embodies examples of community by kinship, community of place, and community of mind. Interesting case studies are used throughout.

SEYMOUR SARASON (1995) provides honest commentary on the need for radical change in the governance structures and power relationships in school systems. In his book titled *Parental Involvement and the Political Principle: Why the Existing Governance*

*Structure of Schools Should Be Abolished,* published by Jossey-Bass (San Francisco) he argues for radical changes that would give all constituents a greater voice in decision-making. Three areas of focus are (1) the moral, conceptual, and practical significance of the political process; (2) a rationale for abolishing the existing governance structure of school systems; and (3) a discussion of what is the most important purpose by which schools should be judged.

# 2

# RESPONDING TO CHANGE

## AN INVITATION . . .

In this chapter we invite the reader to consider how the management and control of time, resources, and curriculum in schools seriously inhibit change. As schools tend to be managed, so too are attempts at change. Overtures toward change have historically concerned themselves with "things": kits, programs, packages, and so on, all designed to achieve specific outcomes.

**How might approaches to change emanate from beliefs and understandings of people?**

The practice of asking "why" seems to be missing from traditional approaches to change and innovation. Two things are in need of attention: (1) change based on a deep understanding of young people and their learning needs, and (2) an ethic of caring that honors and respects this deep understanding. Striving for deeper meaning and understanding demands different ways of responding to change. Past practice of focusing on "things" needs to be reviewed to focus on people. Change would provide opportunities to reflect on practice in ongoing, seamless ways, resulting in continuous development of people and schools.

Conditions within schools would require a sharing of leadership and decision making among all constituents. Power and control would be shared, traditional hierarchical arrangements discontinued. Teaching would be understood for its essential morality. In this regard schools would see young people in the process of *becoming* rather than *having*.

&#10087;   &#10087;   &#10087;

&#10087; EVERY YEAR AROUND MARCH, our thoughts turn to the next school year and some form of planning takes place. As an administrative team, we decided to have a school planning retreat. Next year was going to be one of change, so we thought getting out of the city would foster the necessary collaborative environment. It was to be a time to open our minds and share possibilities with one another.

Our school was situated in a low socioeconomic area with a diverse, multicultural student population. Students suffered from low self-esteem and poor relationship skills. In the face of these difficulties, we asked ourselves if we were truly a student-centered school. Through our conversations we uncovered some strong beliefs about students and their learning. We found ourselves constricted and constrained within our current organization.

Our first morning of planning concluded with a decision to form five learning communities. We believed that a community-oriented organization would maximize personal relationships between students and teachers by providing opportunities for people to support, listen to, understand, and care for one another. Each learning community would have five teachers, an administrative team member, and about 140 students. These were the only parameters laid down by the principal. Which teachers would work in each learning community and what grade level a learning community would become was open for discussion.

By the end of the day teachers had been placed in learning communities based on their interests and existing relationships. The next step was to determine how a learning community might operate—what it believed about students and, as a result, how it might organize for learning. The conversation seemed to come to a halt as members of the administrative team turned to the principal and asked for direction. "What's the timetable going to be?" asked one person. The principal indicated that it was the responsibility of the learning community to build a timetable that reflected the attributes and professional strengths of the staff, and that addressed the needs of students.

Questions flowed from the team members: "Who's going to teach math?" "How much time should we give to math?" "Who is going to be the language arts specialist?" "How much time do we need?" "How can physical education operate without physical education specialists?" Some people thought we could cycle all our students out of learning communities to physical education specialists. Others thought the idea didn't fit with their learning communities' notions of "community" and the desire to act as generalists. Many argued that structure was needed. Some demanded a common timetable with subject-area specialists. The conversation continued . . .

----

This story shows how teachers tend to approach change through the eyes of conventional behavior. People seem to move along a path of change readily at first, but when comfort levels are disturbed to the point of dissonance, urges to back away are common. In our story, team members looked to the principal for direction. "Who's going to teach math?" "How can physical education operate without specialists?" Questions were rooted in what *had been* rather than what *might be*. This was in spite of the collective decision to form learning communities, with autonomy to decide how the communities would operate, with the utmost flexibility, to meet the needs of their young people.

## CONVENTIONAL BEHAVIOR IN SCHOOLING

School organization is a telling indicator of how adults and young people co-exist. Previously, we discussed the traditional roots of schooling: industrial practices, factory model, "conveyor belt" mentality, and so on. It is interesting to consider the effect of the forces within a traditional school organization that maintain the status quo. The power of conventional schooling describes the past, dominates the present, and constrains the future. Conventional forces tend to place straitjackets around people, allowing only limited flexibility for creative thinking. Our story points to the power of convention among the teachers, while the principal was encouraging an unfettered consideration of change. A number of the staff were uncomfortable with such license and found it easier to attempt to manage and control student learning.

## Management and Control of Learning

A majority of the learning community leaders seemed more concerned about the management of people, time, resources, and curriculum than the learning needs of young people. Schools attempt to "make" people learn and this breeds an attitude of compliance and dependency. "Making people learn, and making them learn certain things in certain ways, teaches them to abide by decisions from above, instead of learning to think for themselves" (Moffett, 1994, p. 6). "Making" people learn is a product of management. In our story, many of the learning community leaders centered on managing and controlling to the point where innovation and change became the ends rather than the means. These leaders were seeking the predictable toward controlled outcomes. Innovation and change are unpredictable, requiring high tolerance for ambiguity and uncertainty. There was a need among the learning community leaders to make decisions and answer questions immediately. In fact, the very nature of schools as institutions tends to be in opposition to the demands of innovation and change. **What causes people to so quickly own constraints and lose the excitement of possibilities during times of innovation and change?**

❧   ON THE LAST MORNING OF OUR ADMINISTRATIVE RETREAT, we took some time to reflect on the weekend's experience and share our thoughts about the upcoming year. As the learning community leaders shared their thoughts about the weekend, I could tell that any ideas about innovation and flexibility had been suppressed by the need to manage and control the change. One person had already set the timetable and determined who would be teaching each subject. Another leader rambled on about the need to order more science textbooks. The book was going to be the basis for the program and consequently each student needed a text. Another leader spoke about physical education, the sports to be covered, and the mechanism by which the learning community would rotate the students from subject to subject. Cooperative learning, decreed another leader, will be the way we instruct our students.

   I could not help but wonder about the discussions that had taken place over the last two days. We had talked about the characteristics of our students, how they learn best, student voice and choice, flexible organization, and ways of doing things differently to meet the needs of our young people. It seemed as though our talk would have little effect on many people's actions. We did talk a lot that weekend, but will anything really change?

Managing and controlling seemed to be the response to change by many of the learning community leaders. McNeill (1988) helps us make sense of organizations that focus on managing and controlling.

> They fall into a ritual of teaching and learning that tends toward minimal standards and minimal effort. This sets off a vicious cycle. As students disengage from enthusiastic involvement in the learning process, administrators often see the disengagement as a control problem. They then increase their attention to managing students and teachers, rather than supporting their instructional purpose. (p. xviii)

In our story there seemed to be a tendency to relive this vicious cycle. Each leader was to act as "the principal" of his or her learning community. Each began to live out traditional stories of what it means to be a principal. Now in positions of power, they appeared to be seeking the predictable to arrive efficiently and effectively at the known. In living out this role of "the principal," the value was in the task completion, as evidenced by the learning community leader who had completed the timetable and slotted in the students and teachers. This control over timetable, teaching assignments, and curriculum was exercised through power, with little regard for the affected people. Doesn't this deny liberation? Unless teachers are liberated to harness their collective wisdom, experience, and professional knowledge, and to apply their insights toward the greater success of the schools in which they work, then schooling is unlikely to benefit from enduring progress and change. Most of the learning communities discussed in the stories were geared to the management of learning: clinically managing people, resources, and time in the belief that such efficiency would equate to successful learning for young people. Whose interests were being served in these learning communities? One leader indicated that instruction would be based on a cooperative learning approach. How could such a statement be made without input from other stakeholders such as colleagues, parents, and students? Was it because *cooperative learning* was the buzz word, the fad of the time, or the thing to do to gain recognition?

## FOCUS ON PEOPLE AS OPPOSED TO THINGS

Coombs (1988) presents an interesting perspective when he points to our persistent practice of focusing on "things". The project, package, kit, trend, series, or particular innovation essentially become ends in themselves. Schools tend to drift, amorphously, from "thing" to "thing," from trend to trend, with the one great binding factor being the steady, regularized ways of doing things. It is this incredibly powerful force of regularized practice that continues to impede change in our schools. The powerful habit of wanting to implement something to get things moving in a school tends to mark our behavior. Teachers and administrators have been encouraged to place their time and energy into implementing the "thing." Perhaps, as in our stories, retreats have been planned, conferences attended, and in-services conducted. In-school coordinators may have been appointed much like the learning community leaders.

Seldom, however, do decisions to implement the "things" emanate from deep understandings of the learning needs of young people. The things—series, packages, kits, programs, and so on—are themselves *managerial systems,* often complete with instructions and tests. Teacher needs become the sole criterion for use. Understanding, based on student learning needs, may be a distant consideration. What was motivating the teachers in our story as they considered the learning community concept? Perhaps the orientations toward control and management, embedded in the conventions of traditional schooling, deny meaning and understanding through the interests of young people. We wonder whether this orientation isn't responsible for some of the difficulties we get into when discussing and defending schooling with our constituents. **How might parents respond if the case for changes in schooling was framed around clear understandings of the needs of young people?**

---

WE AWAIT THE PARENT–TEACHER CONFERENCES with Mrs. Sharples with some apprehension. Mrs. Sharples is so concerned about her daughter's education; she wants her to be successful socially and academically. "How many new science concepts do you think Ashley has learned this semester?" "Ms. Connors, are you sure that with this integrated stuff the students get exposed to enough science?" "I don't see Ashley working on much physics at home. Is she going to be behind once she moves on to high school?" And, "If Ashley is constantly getting 95% in math, why is she not doing harder work to challenge her abilities?" These are some tough questions from a concerned parent. Teachers are uncomfortable talking to Mrs. Sharples because she asks difficult questions. You have to have a deep understanding of Ashley's progress to respond. When Mrs. Sharples has asked all her questions and has understood our responses, she is supportive of the work we do. She needs to be listened to and heard. Perhaps, instead of being apprehensive, we should look forward to speaking with parents like her, to reflect on our beliefs and practices.

---

Mrs. Sharples was seeking to understand her child's world. Shouldn't parents be asking "why" questions? "Why are you using this material?" "Why are you using these particular learning and teaching strategies?" In the story, the questions Mrs. Sharples asked initially led to dissonance and discomfort on the part of the teacher. However, do we not have a moral and professional responsibility to respond to parental inquiry? By honoring Mrs. Sharples' concerns, the teacher was able to deepen her understanding of what she was doing and why. We can begin to do this by:

- uncovering assumptions about schooling
- reflecting on our work and forging open, trusting relationships

## Uncovering Assumptions

Newman (1987) challenges teachers to uncover assumptions that describe practice. She raises questions about tacitness. Senge (1993) and Sergiovanni (1993) speak of mental models and mindscapes, respectively, as often being held tacitly. They influence how we respond to our world, help shape and determine our actions, and describe our beliefs about learning, teaching, and school organization. **In what ways could "why" questions asked by students, colleagues, parents, and ourselves, help us to more clearly understand and shape our mental models and mindscapes?** The teacher learned to genuinely value the type of questions Mrs. Sharples asked when she began to see the conference as a mutual learning experience. If we are truthful about our decisions and behaviors, then an honest dissatisfaction may arise between our beliefs and our actions. As our mental models, or *mindscapes,* are uncovered and challenged we may find that what for each of us is at the heart of education—our beliefs—are not lived out in our daily lives in school. This is what makes it such a risk to examine our beliefs, and listen to and ask "why" questions. Perhaps this is why many of us feel uncomfortable when parents like Mrs. Sharples ask challenging questions. The teacher saw the questions as opportunities, not only to enhance the relationship with Mrs. Sharples and Ashley, but also to understand her beliefs as they were storied in classroom life.

## Reflection and Openness

The more we talk, reflect, and question, the better we will be at making sense of our work in schools. The conversation that the teacher and Mrs. Sharples shared was an important opportunity for reflection and the beginning of an open and trusting relationship. In many cases parents admonish schools for working in new ways simply because the methods are different than those used when they went to school. Mrs. Sharples was concerned about this "integrated stuff" probably because the thematic approach was unfamiliar. She needed to talk with the teacher, to be heard and responded to in a genuine and caring way. Noddings (1992) writes, "Good teaching starts with the construction of trusting relationships and works continually to build on the foundation of trust" (p. xii). We wonder if parents who develop this type of relationship by asking questions and becoming involved soon move from admonishing innovation to becoming strong advocates for change. Challenge is an essential, but sensitive, practice. Mrs. Sharples pursued her "why" questions with a certain tenacity, but without persistent inquiry to uncover the reasons for practice, a danger exists of educators pressing on, regardless, with whatever it is they would like to do. **To what extent does the essence of change for parents, teachers, and students lie in the development of meaning and understanding through trusting relationships?**

---

❧ I WAS NEW TO THE PRINCIPALSHIP of my elementary/junior high school and my enthusiasm was at a peak. Most of my recent experience had been in junior high school, so I began to think about strategies for working with elementary teachers. "Go for the jugular," I thought, "work with first grade!"

I spoke with the first-grade teacher and suggested that I might work with her in the classroom in a kind of team-teaching initiative.

I had never taught young children before and my first visits were mainly for observation. I was intrigued by the teacher's constant motion and constant change of pace, and the incessant questions from the children. Attention span took on a new meaning. I acquired a tremendous admiration for my colleague and wondered how she had energy at the end of the day for other aspects of her life.

Time passed and I began to feel sensations of confidence. "Perhaps it's time for me to take over the class," I thought. My colleague and I discussed the matter and decided I would begin by spending some time with the first grade class, alone, on the following Monday.

All of us have humbling experiences. One of my most memorable ones came on that Monday morning. I entered the room imbued with enthusiasm. Selective memory has faded the lesson-plan detail but I remember, painfully, speaking to the children. Suddenly, one child stood up and went to play with a curtain at the rear of the room. "Jimmy", I said with the customary altered tone of voice, "Why aren't you sitting in your seat listening?"

"I don't like what you're saying, so I'm going to play with the curtains," he replied. Ego is a fragile thing and mine had just become more fragile. I was but minutes into my lesson when I had already lost one of the class. Authority brought Jimmy back and the lesson continued.

By this time, Joany and Kim were sitting on the floor in the back of the room admiring the flowers on Kim's dress. The pattern of behavior was apparent. Pangs of desperation came over me in waves—huge waves! Tidal waves! Help!

Young children have yet to learn the "game" of school. They are so naturally curious and honest that structure and control are not understood. Should I control them through authority to conform to my structure? Or should I adjust myself to free their honesty and curiosity toward unfettered learning?

---

This new principal, in spite of valuable time spent with the first-grade teacher, began his new venture with practice rooted in his past. Clearly, old assumptions—no doubt tacit assumptions—were driving his decision making. He had not adequately considered the cardinal rule: Learning comes before teaching. The task of a teacher is to invite young people to learn. As a teacher it is advisable to engage in a personal, professional assessment of the young people you are about to teach, with regard to their nature as young people and the ways of learning they naturally prefer. Unless these matters are considered and embraced in planning for learning before decisions about teaching are made, we may well be forced into the use of power and authority to "make" and "tell" students to learn. Our principal might be accused of this folly. The asking of "why" and reflection on the reasons for engaging in particular practice, are often vexingly absent in schools. Even our well-intentioned principal was somewhat lacking. The missing element is what might be termed the *philosophical challenge*.

A group of people, whose leaders were planning to institute practices that would profoundly affect the lives of other human beings, were pondering their plans. One among the group questioned the leaders' actions. His colleagues responded, impatiently, to his challenging questions.

- We're not interested in all those verbal distinctions here, this isn't a university seminar.
- We don't want all this theory, we have a practical job to do.
- We haven't got time to look at first principles, we just want to make the thing work.
- Words and concepts are just man-made anyway, what can you prove from them.
- Well, like it or not, it's not our business to argue about this, we don't make policy, we have to take it as given.
- If you don't like it, then you can get out, but stop trying to persuade us that it's wrong. Each man has his own opinion about what's right and wrong, there's no point arguing about it. (Wilson, 1983, p. 191)

These comments were extracted from Nazi archives during the period when gas chambers were being constructed. One member of a relevant committee objected. He questioned the meaning of "non-Aryan," tried to distinguish between mental health and politics and asked his colleagues to consider the correctness of killing people with whom they disagreed. Now, this is a rather severe case to cite in a discussion of schooling, but there is one similarity—lack of reflection. It is striking that lack of reflection tends to survive almost any situation, however horrific it may seem in retrospect. We in schooling are also concerned with practices which affect the lives of human beings. **To what extent do we reflect on the learning we are inviting our young people to experience in our schools?**

Educational philosophers are frequently given short shrift by their colleagues in schools. Wilson (1983) explains that the philosopher "merely asks people to consider whether they are doing, or meaning, A or B; whether their aims are clear, admirable, disastrous, wicked, muddled, or whatever. The philosopher simply interrogates" (p. 191). *Interrogates* is a strong word to use, particularly in light of the adversarial conditions existing in the world at the time of the Nazi archive reference, but Wilson's point is germane. Mrs. Sharples, in a more benign way, was "interrogating." She was asking whether the teacher was doing A or B. She was seeking to understand the teacher's aims. The principal, on the other hand, was proceeding without interrogation. He could clearly have benefited from the philosophical challenge.

Could it be that one of the reasons we are often unsuccessful in implementing change is that we focus on things instead of people? As such we lack a deep understanding of young people and the way they see their world. "Why" questions, like the ones Mrs. Sharples asked, help peel away the layers covering the assumptions and beliefs at the heart of our work. It is not until we peel back these layers that we will be able to base change on a deep understanding of young people and the ethic of care required for this understanding to be honored and respected.

&#x223D;   I GOT TO KNOW NANCY BEST when she moved to the south side of the city with her dad. I often drove her to school. Her mom was in a drug rehabilitation center and her dad provided shelter, food, and safety, but little love and affection. We talked about boys, music, homework, and fashion.

I'll never forget the Friday morning Nancy appeared in the library where I was attending a leadership team meeting. I could see her small body shaking and a horrible combination of fear, sadness, and anxiety on her face. When I reached her, she collapsed into my arms. We hugged and held hands for a long time before her story spilled out. She had found out that a past boyfriend had tested positive for HIV. She was sure she had it and was going to die. She didn't want anyone else to know and was hoping I would take her to be tested. I took her out to my car, turned on the heater, and played our favorite tape. I ran back into school to be sure my team of teachers could cover my classes. Nancy calmed down enough, with the motion of the car and rhythm of the music, to prepare her for the explicit and personal questions that would be asked of her at the clinic.

Soon we sat together, her hand gripping mine. We were called into the nurse's office. I heard Nancy answer "yes" to having been sexually abused as a child. I heard her say she had been sexually active and had not used any form of birth control since she was twelve. Shortly after the test was done we went out for a late breakfast and then condom shopping. We managed a few smiles over breakfast and some giggles in the family planning aisle of the drugstore. We found ourselves back in the same waiting room for the results. When the nurse said the results were negative, I breathed a sigh of relief and Nancy asked, "is that good?"

"It's good, Nancy, it's good!"

This story certainly reflects societal change and the difficult, sometimes painful, situations in which young people find themselves. How can we as educators respond to such changes? We were again reminded of Bateson's (1990) view of family life providing metaphors for broader ethical relations. Nancy was a poignant example.

## An Ethic of Care

The notably altered complexion of family life and the palpable complexity of society is a volatile milieu for most people, but for young people it is often a struggle. Without care, compassion, and nurturing relationships, children are particularly susceptible to harm. Nancy and her teacher, Tina, obviously have a deep and important relationship. How did this come about? Could it be that Tina's focus on the people, humanness, and morality of schooling—and not on the things, management, and organization—is the starting point for such positive, meaningful relationships?

Noddings (1992) describes such relationships as caring ones. She argues that young people need to be cared for; to be "understood, received, respected, and recognized" (p. xi). The purpose of education, based on Nodding's ethic of care, is to encourage the development of moral, healthy, competent, loving, and caring people. Does this suggest a way of responding to the changes in our world and to the needs of the young people with whom we work? Perhaps seeking to understand our students and their needs, talents, and interests through caring relationships is a way of responding to change. What if Nancy did not have a caring teacher? **Why do we tend to focus on academic achievement, measuring competence, and managing for results at the expense of the morality and humanness of schooling?**

Young people are growing up in a complex world, one that would present a challenge for the most mature adult. How troublesome it must be for our youth. The management orientation that describes schools compounds the difficulties youngsters bring to school from their out-of-school world. "Get to school on time, sit in class and get on with your work." "You are in school to learn and the teacher is in school to teach". There is an insidious expectation in this attitude that students should be able to suppress emotions such as sadness, anxiety, hopelessness, and despair and get on with learning. It is easy to be left with the impression that the only emotions wanted in school are happiness, joy, and enthusiasm, all wrapped in an attitude of compliance. We wonder how many young people, like Nancy, who desperately need care, pass through our education systems with no trusting and caring relationships with their teachers. Work such as this, based on Nodding's ideas of care and caring relationships, has been criticized by some as being nonacademic. But Noddings (1992) argues the following:

> If a school has one main goal, a goal that guides the establishment and priority of all others, it should be to promote the growth of students as healthy, competent, and moral people. . . . We cannot ignore our children—their purposes, anxieties, and relationships—in the service of making them more competent in academic skills. My position is not anti-intellectual. It is a matter of setting priorities. Intellectual development is important, but it cannot be the first priority of schools. (p. 10)

If we want to shift our focus to dealing with our students emotionally as well as academically, we should consider the following factors:

- caring relationships
- power and control
- teacher–student relationships
- the role of voice

## Caring Relationships

We learned many years ago of the need to recognize schools as social institutions (Rutter et al., 1979; Edmunds & Fredericksen, 1979; Goodlad, 1983). Whenever there are hundreds of people working and interacting within the same four walls, for five to six hours a day, there is little choice but to be concerned with the social aspects of their worlds. Learning—all forms of learning—will prosper when it is founded on good relationships. The human spirit thrives on caring and compassion, on esteem and trust. Even adults require these conditions to function fully. Young people—growing, maturing young people—must experience these conditions to learn successfully. Nancy, responding to Tina in a journal they share, describes how these caring relationships have enhanced her academic work:

Dear Nancy,

Sometimes I wonder about our relationship, Nancy. I mean about a "teacher" and a "student" being friends. I think it's great, but is it unusual? I don't ever remember having my old teachers as friends. With only a few did I want to spend time outside of class. What do you think about this? Have the times changed and most teachers in your experience been your friends? What difference does it make, if any, to have a teacher who is a friend?

Love, Tina

Dear Tina,

I remember the first day in Grade 8. We had to sit in the learning community "Relaxation Zone". We were introduced to all the teachers. When I first saw you guys I had no idea that you would become my best friends.

In the beginning I was a young teen not really caring about the teachers the way I do now. I remember the first time I saw David Reardon. I thought he was kind of cute and as the days and months went by I began to have a crush on him. So there I was, a few months into Grade 8 and having a ball, until, of course, I went home. I hated going home. I wanted to stay at school, where I wasn't being abused, mentally and physically.

Now it's the end of Grade 9 and times have changed so very much from the beginning of Grade 8. So many of us have grown up. I'm smarter, older, and a little taller. The most important thing is that I have grown very close to my teachers and now they are just like my normal friends. Many of my student friends say that it is so hard to believe that I'm so close to my teachers. I guess in a way it's true because I was never this close with any other teachers. The relationship with my other teachers was always "student" and "teacher", maybe because they didn't want to get to know their students.

In your last journal entry you asked me several questions. I always think about our relationship, it is kind of weird, but just because we are labeled "teacher" and "student" doesn't mean we have to have limits to our relationship. . . . None of my teachers before were my friends. I was just a student and their job was to teach me and that was it. To have a teacher as your friend changes in the sense that I have more respect for you. I listen and work better in class because you guys are my friends, and I hate my friends being mad at me.

Love, Nancy

July 13

Dear Nancy

. . . you said that a lot of people think you are weird for having teachers who are your friends. Well a lot of teachers think I'm weird for having students for friends. But if you really do work and listen more, then doesn't caring for each other make for a better education? Isn't being friends a good thing? Why, I ask, are we the "weird" ones?

Love, Tina

July 14

Dear Tina

. . . I think if all the teachers were as great as you, more kids would try harder in school, because they know that the teachers really care about them. Being friends is such a great thing. We have fun together and you're a great role model for me. Maybe people think we're "weird" because they never had a chance to get close to their students or teachers. . . . The more I think about it, the more I think we're not really "student" and "teacher" anymore. Actually, the only time I call you "teacher" is when I'm trying to explain our relationship to someone. . . .

Love, Nancy

Nancy and Tina have developed a relationship that promotes growth in morality, competence, health, and caring that Noddings espouses. These short excerpts from the journal (which in its entirety focuses on their personal experiences, both in and out of school) demonstrates the value of caring relationships. Nancy feels cared for. Through written and oral conversations, she has reflected on questions of ethics and health, and has "tried harder" in school. It seems obvious, at least to Nancy and Tina, that this caring is essential. Not only is it essential for their relationship but also, according to Noddings, a person learns to be caring through being cared for. The more we model caring with our young people, the more likely they are to be caring people themselves.

The relationship shared by Nancy and Tina contributed to Nancy's achievement. Does academic learning benefit when it is founded on moral and caring relationships among teachers and young people? Because we believe that these relationships are valuable and important, what can we do to encourage their development? In the journal excerpts both Tina and Nancy put the words "student" and "teacher" in quotation marks. The way we make sense of this is that they are words that indicate a hierarchical relationship. At one point Nancy says, " . . . I was just a student . . . " Trusting and caring relationships do not flourish in an atmosphere of power and control. **Why is it that the institution of schooling has grown from and continues to exude behaviors within learning, teaching, and organization, which are based in power and control?**

## Power and Control

Programs of study, resources, and teaching manuals often dictate teaching behavior. Students are compelled to learn required work with intimidating remarks such as, "This is worth 30% on the report card," "Do this tonight or you will face a detention," "If this isn't done by tomorrow you will lose 10%," "If this work isn't finished you will stay in for recess," "Do you want to miss phys. ed.?" and so on. School organizations are managed to the point at which both teachers and students tend to respond with less enthusiasm (McNeil, 1988). Instead of these tendencies toward authority and control, we need to strive to understand the needs of young people and value their ideas and gifts. From this understanding comes our response to internal and external change. Unfortunately, methods and techniques for curriculum, instruction, and classroom management dominate the responses to change in education. These responses do not value individuals—students or teachers—they are merely mechanisms and behaviors to be modified and tinkered with to produce a mildly altered status quo.

〰 THE BIG ROOM, OUR TRIPLE-SIZE CLASSROOM, is the heart of our school wing, in much the same way as the kitchen is often the heart of a family home. It is the first place teachers and students go in the morning to talk over coffee and breakfast. The big room even has a fridge, microwave, kettle, and toaster for anyone to use. Six teachers share this school wing and we team teach our 150 students. The big room contains all our desks and many tables and chairs, is fully carpeted, and has a corner with comfortable couches and arm chairs. The couch area has been dubbed the Relaxation Zone. This is where we sit with the students, in the morning and at lunch, to just talk about our lives. It is also a place where we most often meet with our student "ministers," to talk about ways of improving, changing, and shaping the work we do together. During our common preparation time we all gravitate to the Relaxation Zone to consider the days behind and ahead of us. We talk about our successes and concerns and ask ourselves why certain approaches worked while others did not. We share conversations we have had with our students, parents, and colleagues and wonder what our responses should be. It is a safe place to agree, disagree, argue, debate, question, dream, and wonder. I suppose the Relaxation Zone isn't really all that relaxing, but I guess it depends on your definition of the word!

What happens in the Big Room and the Relaxation Zone that might make it a place conducive to change? We believe a key factor to be the talk among students and teachers.

## Teacher-Student Relationships

Schools need to provide settings for students and teachers to talk about their lives and their work. These settings could provide some conditions for teachers to learn what is happening in the lives of students, to talk with one another about educational issues and to determine possible responses to enact changes. The Big Room was where the teachers met during all their prep times, to reflect on their experiences, question their practice, share their stories, and determine ways of working that meet student needs. We are reminded of Warren-Little's (1981) operational definition of *collegiality* as the presence of four behaviors: that teachers (1) talk continuously about their practice, (2) observe each other engaged in their work, (3) work together on curriculum, and (4) teach each other what they know about learning and teaching. It seems that this is the type of relationship shared by the teachers in the story as they work together in the Big Room. Such collaboration fosters a higher level of morale, trust, and learning. We begin to make meaning and construct knowledge, processes that give us confidence to take new risks and be open to change.

"When teachers observe, examine, question, and reflect on their ideas and develop new practices which lead toward their ideals, students are alive. When teachers stop growing, so do their students." (Barth, 1990, p. 33) Barth states eloquently how important it is for teachers to be learners, not only for their own sake, but also for the sake of the young people with whom they work. The Big Room story serves as a reminder of Barth's (1990) writing about a community of learners, where adults and children learn together to solve problems and ask questions that are important to them.

"In a community of learners, adults and children learn simultaneously and in the same place to think critically and analytically and to solve problems that are important to them. In a community of learners, learning is endemic and mutually visible." (Barth, 1990, p. 45) Our students are not going to believe that we value their voice if we are not perceived as learners who will think about and respond to their questions and concerns. The voices of young people must be valued by educators; it is for young people that we need to change and improve. Places like the Big Room, where formal and informal meetings occur with students and teachers, are important if we are to improve what we do in school.

&#x223d; PARENT–TEACHER INTERVIEWS had become routine, ritualized, and mechanical. The ambience was cold. Our school improvement process saw the staff in review teams, each with a different school dimension as a focus. In an attempt to rejuvenate the parent–teacher interview process, the staff decided that the school dimension team, with a focus on learning, would take a leadership role in exploring alternatives. It was clear to all that no decision about an alternative would be taken until all the staff had the opportunity to discuss the matter thoroughly, and that each dimension team would consider the effect of a decision on the school, through its particular focus.

The first meeting in which the learning dimension team reported to staff was at first calm, later tense, and finally fractious. Staff members who had been comfortable and secure in their established territories, were hearing suggestions that would disrupt their world. The interests of students and parents were less important than those of the teachers. Some staff members, on hearing proposals that students should accompany parents to the interviews, became agitated: "There are some things we just can't say when students are present." "Students will be very uncomfortable." The learning dimension team members were uncomfortable at this point. The young teacher leading the discussion was becoming visibly distressed. As a principal, what should I do? Jump in and take over? Rescue the team? Terminate the discussion in the hope that reason and calm would prevail another day? No, those urges were suppressed out of confidence and trust that the team in question and the staff in general could deal with the situation. Probing questions, rather than authority-laden statements, were preferred. "Help me understand why you. . . . " How do you think the parent would feel if . . . ?" "Whose interests are being served by . . . ?" "What do you think would happen if . . . ?"

Next day, in the staff room and in the halls, conversation was rich. Interestingly, the focus of this talk was on the feelings of colleagues as much as it was on substance of positions taken: "I felt really sorry for Jane; some of us weren't very kind to her." "You know, those people put in a heck of a lot of good work. I don't think we really recognized that." Of course, one or two staff members remained rigid and unbending, but over the succeeding week, a sense of empathy and professionalism seemed to reign.

The next meeting, a week later, and the meeting a week after that, were wonderfully productive. Staff members arrived at decisions that established parent–teacher–student interviews, in a library environment with carpet on the floors, plants and wall decorations for atmosphere, refreshments served by young people, and hosts to welcome and usher families to convivial waiting areas.

I believe all of us on that staff, particularly those on the learning dimension team, became richer for the experience, benefiting from the freedom and trust to allow decision-making its due course—turbulence notwithstanding.

---

This story, as in the Big Room story, describes a setting that allowed for successful change. What was important about this setting? We believe the idea of voice, in this case the voices of Jane and the other teachers, is important.

## The Role of Voice

Voice is the meaning that resides in the individual and enables that individual to participate in a community. . . . The struggle for voice begins when a person attempts to communicate meaning to someone else. Finding the words, speaking for oneself, and feeling heard are all part of this process. (Britzman, in Clandinin, 1993, p. 2)

Doesn't this describe Jane's experience? She was trying to communicate what parent–teacher interviews meant to her and was hoping that her voice would be heard and valued. What about the other teachers in the story? We suppose they had to struggle with their own voices and think about their knowledge of parent–teacher interviews. Eventually they learned to make room for each other, to hear one another's voices and to understand that in those voices were ways of making sense of themselves and their work. How important was the action of the principal in this story? What would have happened had he terminated the discussion, or made the decision himself? What would the principal have done in a traditional, hierarchical role? We believe the use of questions helped create a space in which the voices of all were valued. Questions lead to reflection, examination, and dialogue on the part of the staff, which eventually improved relationships and staff morale, and set the stage for continuous improvement.

In Chapter 1 we considered the changing world and how changes are lived out in our lives and the lives of young people. We presented stories, questions, and musings of our experiences at the beginning of that journey. In this chapter we are concerned about the schools' response to the changing world. We question why so often change is found in the implementation of new techniques, programs, or packages, rather than within people themselves. When the focus is on people, one discovers a process of learning, reflection, dialogue, and deep understanding as the foundation for change and continuous school growth. This process and dialogue includes the voices of many people, like the administrators on their retreat, parents like Mrs. Sharples, students like Nancy and the ones who gather in the Big Room, and teachers like Jane. If schools are places where we do value the voices of others, where reflection and dialogue are part of the milieu, and where the process is directed by genuine care for the young people with whom we work, we will have schools in which growth is continuous and the learning is rich.

# AN INVITATION TO THE READER

The following page suggests a process for thinking about the chapter, to stimulate conversation, encourage debate, share stories, provoke further questions, challenge current thinking, or engage in further personal reflection. University classes, professional development groups, school staffs, and parent groups may find the chapter's questions and related text useful, as a challenge to personal beliefs, understandings and experiences, toward affirmation or change.

We present the concept of "filter." Readers are invited to consider the central question of the chapter, along with the questions that arise from the text. It is not our intention to limit or reduce context to one small portion of the chapter—we are conscious of the problem of reductionism. It is our hope that, as readers proceed through the book, they will respond to questions in a more holistic manner.

The concept of filter is a metaphor for the reader's personal beliefs, values, and experiences, through which new ideas are explored and current beliefs challenged. It is this filtering that provides an opportunity for the reader to make personal connections to the questions and ideas in the chapter. This process may provide an opportunity to deepen meaning and understanding of the concepts and ideas discussed.

**In the following framework, you are invited to contemplate your beliefs, understandings, and experiences through reflecting on the questions and related text in Chapter 2.**

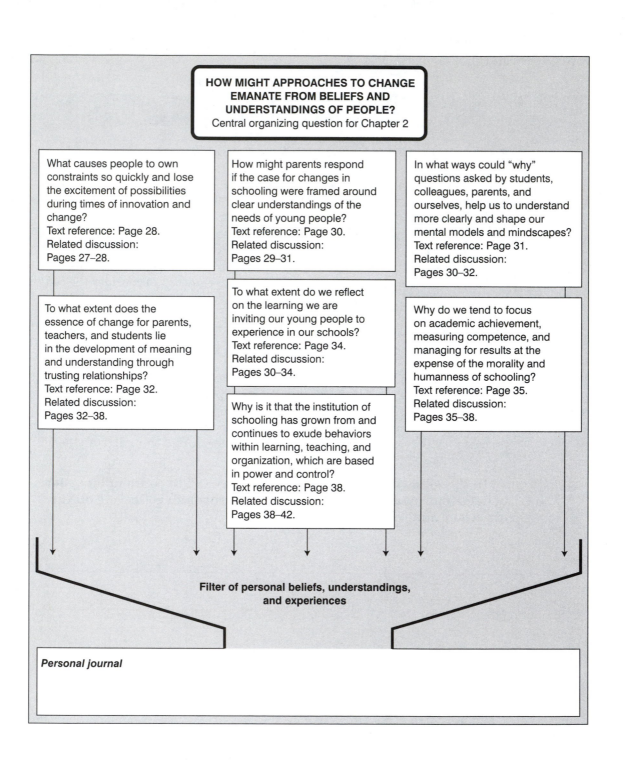

**HOW MIGHT APPROACHES TO CHANGE EMANATE FROM BELIEFS AND UNDERSTANDINGS OF PEOPLE?**
Central organizing question for Chapter 2

What causes people to own constraints so quickly and lose the excitement of possibilities during times of innovation and change?
Text reference: Page 28.
Related discussion:
Pages 27–28.

How might parents respond if the case for changes in schooling were framed around clear understandings of the needs of young people?
Text reference: Page 30.
Related discussion:
Pages 29–31.

In what ways could "why" questions asked by students, colleagues, parents, and ourselves, help us to understand more clearly and shape our mental models and mindscapes?
Text reference: Page 31.
Related discussion:
Pages 30–32.

To what extent does the essence of change for parents, teachers, and students lie in the development of meaning and understanding through trusting relationships?
Text reference: Page 32.
Related discussion:
Pages 32–38.

To what extent do we reflect on the learning we are inviting our young people to experience in our schools?
Text reference: Page 34.
Related discussion:
Pages 30–34.

Why do we tend to focus on academic achievement, measuring competence, and managing for results at the expense of the morality and humanness of schooling?
Text reference: Page 35.
Related discussion:
Pages 35–38.

Why is it that the institution of schooling has grown from and continues to exude behaviors within learning, teaching, and organization, which are based in power and control?
Text reference: Page 38.
Related discussion:
Pages 38–42.

**Filter of personal beliefs, understandings, and experiences**

*Personal journal*

# REFERENCES

Barth, R. (1990). *Changing schools from within*. San Francisco: Jossey-Bass.

Bateson, M. C. (1980). *Composing a life*. New York: Atlantic Monthly Press.

Clandinin, J. (1993). *Learning to teach, teaching to learn*. New York: Teachers' College Press

Coombs, A. (1988) New assumptions for educational reform. *Educational Leadership, 45*(5), 38–40.

Edmunds, R., & Fredericksen, J. (1979). *Search for effective schools: The identification and analysis of city schools that are instructionally effective for poor children*. Cambridge, MA: Center for Urban Schools, Harvard University.

Goodlad, J. (1983). *A place called school*. New York: McGraw-Hill.

McNeil, L. (1988*). Contradictions of control*. New York: Routledge.

Moffett, J. (1994). *The universal schoolhouse: A spiritual awakening*. San Francisco: Jossey-Bass.

Newman, J. (1987, November). Learning to teach by uncovering our assumptions. *Language Arts, 67*(7), 727–737.

Noddings, N. (1992). *The challenge to care in schools*. New York: Teachers' College Press.

Rutter, M., et al. (1979*). Fifteen thousand hours: Secondary schools and their effects on children*. Cambridge, MA: Harvard University Press.

Senge, P. (1994*). The fifth discipline: The art and practice of the learning organization*. New York: Currency Doubleday.

Sergiovanni, T. (1992*). Moral leadership: Getting to the heart of school improvement*. San Francisco: Jossey-Bass.

Warren-Little, J. (1981). The persistence of privacy: Autonomy and initiative in teachers' professional relations. *Teachers' College Record, 91*(4), 509–536.

Wilson, J. (1983, May). Reflections: A letter from Oxford. *Harvard Educational Review, 53*(2), 188–193.

# SUGGESTED READINGS

A book of selected papers and excerpts from books by SEYMOUR SARASON (1995) may provide the reader with further interesting insights into educational change. *School Change: The Personal Development of a Point of View,* published by Teachers' College Press (New York), addresses topics such as the school culture and the process of change, the purpose of schooling and changes in governance and power in the politics of education. A particular theme that may be of interest posits that individuals cannot change settings without first experiencing or participating in that setting.

NANCY DANA (1995) presents a useful article titled, "Action Research, School Change, and the Silencing of Teacher Voice," in the *Action in Teacher Education Journal (16)*4,

59–70. The paper documents findings from collaborative action research involving the author and four elementary school teachers to explore, implement and document practitioner initiated change. Of particular note to the reader may be the discussion of how peers and principals can silence teachers voices.

MICHAEL FULLAN (1996) discusses "overload and fragmentation" as factors that often combine to reduce motivation in educators as they pursue reform and change. His article, "Turning Systemic Thinking on its Head", in *Phi Delta Kappan 77*(6), 420–423, posits that existing school cultures and structures are antithetically opposed to systemic reform, because they contradict educational change, which is essentially nonlinear.

BYRD JONES and ROBERT MALOY (1996) invite readers to envision new schools for the emerging Information Age. Their book, titled *Schools for an Information Age: Reconstructing Foundations for Learning and Teaching* (ERIC reference #ED 396023) argues that the narrative that made sense of industrial progress has been broken and that it is no longer unquestionable that academic achievement will bring higher income and a satisfying life. All chapters are useful, but the conclusion, which discusses empowering students for the Information Age, is particularly germane.

# 3

# HUMANNESS OF THE LEARNER

## AN INVITATION . . .

Our discussion continues with an invitation to examine the ways that young people have been viewed and treated in schools and the hopes they might realistically hold for their place in the future. Learners have certainly been affected by the hierarchical structure of educational institutions—their place being near the bottom. A traditional focus, in which the power and control lie with the teacher and those "above," leaves little room for authentic student decision making, creative problem solving, or any sense of students responsibility and ownership for their education or their school.

**To what extent are learners recognized as complete human beings?**

Teaching is a moral enterprise. When we interact with young people we are intervening in their lives. Perhaps we need to pause and contemplate the profoundness of this intervention. The strong ethic of caring demanded as we respect and honor the humanness and voice of the young person calls into question many of the traditional ways of responding to them in schools. If we define young people as already possessing knowledge, as already having ways of presenting themselves to the world, as constantly gaining new experiences on their way to becoming more capable and caring individuals, then many of our school practices could benefit from review.

&#x2767;   &#x2767;   &#x2767;

&#x2767;   A FEW YEARS BACK I had the opportunity to teach in the math department. As I have reflected on that experience, I have begun to see the profound effect it had on the way I view students. A typical lesson would begin with, "OK, class, please sit down and take out your books." From this point I would move into a review of the previous day's homework, followed by the next lesson. Anne was a bright student in one of my classes who did very well on tests but never completed her homework. One time I asked her again where her homework was and her typical response of "It's not done" did not greet me. Instead she quipped, "I understand this stuff so why should I do it for homework?"

"Because it's part of your grade," is about all I could come up with. "Practice makes perfect," I added. Then came the toughest question:

"Why do we have to learn this stuff anyway? Could you give me an example of when you have actually used this, other than when you teach it to us?" I searched for a response. It will be useful in your future rang through my mind, but thankfully I did not say it aloud. The particular unit we were doing did not lend itself to any easy examples. Then I began to think about what it was I was asking my students to do and why. Anne affected my practice greatly.

Are schools simply places where young people learn and adults teach? Anne's teacher was viewing his class as a group of students who were there to learn what he decided they should learn. The assumption reflected in the story is that if young people come into class, take out their books, and pay attention, then learning will occur. Anne challenged this assumption. She requested learning that was relevant to her life. **How might teachers invite learning in ways that respect the humanness of the learner?** Perhaps teachers need to reflect on and ask questions about their definition of young people.

1. To what extent are students viewed as passive recipients of knowledge?
2. Are students dependent on teacher direction?
3. Do students possess sufficient experience upon which to make decisions about their lives?
4. Are students capable of taking on authentic responsibility?
5. Do we consider learning to be an accumulation of prescribed knowledge?

## INDEPENDENCE, OWNERSHIP, AND VOICE

Traditionally power and control lie with the teacher. Little room is left for authentic student decision making and creative problem solving. Similarly, students have little opportunity to assume responsibility and ownership for their education and for their school. In Chapter 1 we discussed traditional power relationships in schools, the lack of student responsibility and ownership, and the regularization of school routines and practices. Pressures from the wider community cause teachers to be preoccupied with test scores and covering the curriculum. The ways we define young people tend to be shaped by these traditional forces. Seldom do teachers reveal themselves as human beings to young people, nor do they give young people the opportunity to reveal themselves as human beings. Our story shows how a student's questions can lead to a teacher gaining a deeper understanding of the learning needs and dispositions of students. **How are young people defined and treated in schools?**

"MR. COLDRICK, WE HAVE A NEAT IDEA. We want to go on a walk-a-thon around Alberta to raise money to fight AIDS." Two very excited young people were standing before their principal wanting affirmation for their project. It was February.

"Why don't you sit down and tell me more about it," I suggested, feeling a little pressured to move out into the hallways to see how lunchtime was progressing. Their exuberance fairly bubbled.

"We'd like to start in July as soon as school is out for the summer." They took a big breath. "We're not going away until the second week of August and Deb's family isn't going until a few days after us so the timing is perfect. We could take about four weeks to do the walk have a little rest and be ready to go away with our families knowing that we'd raised a lot of money for a really good cause and maybe even save some lives." If you are like me, you're probably feeling exhausted just reading this! So I interjected with a few questions if for no other reason than to allow the girls to settle down a little. I'm sure they had been thinking about their "neat idea" for some time. Their decision to approach the principal was indicative of two things: They had reached a zenith of excitement and the idea was extremely important to them. I would be less than honest if I didn't admit that I thought their idea was a little unrealistic. The walk around Alberta, according to their plans, would have been a distance of some 1,600 kilometers. They had allowed themselves about four weeks for the actual walk-a-thon and about four-and-a-half months for planning. During that four-and-a-half months they would have to arrange for sponsors, organize logistics for the walk—support vehicles, accommodations, food, rest stops, routes, and so on—and pay some attention to fitness and readiness. There were, as one can imagine, myriad other matters in need of attention.

On Monday of the following week we began our strategy planning. The girls and I met in a classroom at lunchtime, in front of a large blackboard and started to design a plan for organizing their walk-a-thon. Where to begin?

"I think we should go down to the AIDS Calgary office and speak with the director," Debbie said.

"Great idea," Andrea replied. "They will be able to give us information, maybe some support, and they could tell us how they could use all the money we're going to get for them." So the visit to AIDS Calgary became the first item on our planning chart. The girls set up the appointment and four days later we got into my car and off we went to AIDS Calgary.

We met quite a few times in the next four weeks, always during their lunch periods, and tried to bring the "neat idea" to fruition. But the girls came to realize that it wasn't going to be. It was just too big an undertaking. They realized that there were other less ambitious, but equally useful ways of helping AIDS Calgary. Fund-raising in the school, supporting local events, and volunteering were a few.

Was it necessary to spend this time with the two girls on what seemed an unrealistic exercise? I'm sure their bubble could have been popped gently. But these were two young people with a dream that was perhaps the most important thing in the world to them at the time. They had approached a respected adult with a special request: "Please share our dream." As adults we will never be asked to do anything more important. The only thing I could do was to share their dream and help them realize that dream to its conclusion. And they learned a lot!

---

We believe Mr. Coldrick understood his responsibilities to be profound. He knew that through his actions he was intervening in the lives of Debbie and

Andrea. His concern for these two young students, as human beings, demanded that he act out of real concern for their interests. He knew that learning, to be truly a shared experience, must be a mutual experience—that students must be invited to learn.

## Invitational Learning

Teachers who "direct" learning do not "invite" learning with a true sense of mutuality. Directed learning presents an intervention into the lives of young people with troublesome moral questions; it does not invite young people to learn but tends to "tell" them to learn, or at its most troublesome, to "make" them learn. The mutuality of invitational learning engages the true spirit of morality. Not only are the young people experiencing learning, the teacher, as adult and co-learner, shares the experience in a caring and sensitive way. Debbie and Andrea were intervening in Mr. Coldrick's life and he, sensing the mutuality of the occasion, responded with care, sensitivity, and respect. It would have been easy for Mr. Coldrick to have engaged in pleasantries and, after a discreet period of time, sent the girls on their way with paternal dispatch. But he did not. He sensed the profoundness of the moment. He saw beyond the adolescent exuberance to "two young people with a dream that was perhaps the most important thing in their world at the time". **How often do we dismiss young people when they appeal for our interest?**

Managing large numbers of students is difficult. How can we possibly give quality time to every young person who crosses our path? It is, perhaps, a question of disposition. It is certainly a matter of caring. If we respect young people as human beings, if we truly pay attention to what this means, then we will be disposed to respect every attempt they make to share their learning with us, to intervene in our lives, to share their dreams. From the first-grade child who wants to tell about his special trip to his grandma's house to the teen-ager who obliquely alludes to a special purchase at the electronics store, all young people are offering invitations to share their lives.

Debbie and Andrea had a dream which was important to them. Mr. Coldrick sensed the dream and cared sufficiently to accept the invitation. **In what ways do organizational arrangements, teaching methods, and facility use prevent young people from sharing dreams and, more important, prevent teachers from establishing relationships that encourage mutual responses?**

## BUILDING RELATIONSHIPS

Our penchant for management and control of learning and curriculum often precludes the deeper levels of communication, which allow young people to speak from the heart. We have yet to find even the most hardened young person who would not, in the right kind of setting, share some personal feelings. It is in this domain where true learning occurs. How do we open up this domain? **How do we create conditions where relationships develop, where young people are respected as human beings, where intervention into lives is mutual, and where dreams are shared?** The answer surely lies in the belief that teaching is a moral enterprise.

Aoki (1991) speaks about the "inspiriting" of curriculum. In the true sense of curriculum as the totality of learning experiences within a school, *inspiriting* would understand teaching as a moral enterprise. Questions of rightness, fairness, and equity are invoked. This matter of justice, in the context of socialization, demands that we examine altruism: concern for the welfare of others. These kinds of questions and concerns would pervade the building—in the lunchroom, playground, gymnasium, and classroom—such that *all* learning would be founded on moral relationships. In building moral relationships we should consider the following factors:

- equality of humanness
- personalized school environments
- the teacher as friend
- defining young people

## Equality of Humanness

To view young people as people is to bestow on them a humanness which is without degree. From the most exalted statesman to the newborn child, we are equally human. To be human is to be competent, to have a view of the world, and to have ways of dealing with one's life. To interact with another human being is to accept the equality of humanness with humility. But to know humanness is to know who a person is, to know how they see their world. As adults we do this through social banter and telling stories about our peeves, interests, and passions. With young people in schools it is often, "Open your books to page 21 and. . . . " This begins our interactions. **How can we engage in productive interaction without understanding the person or persons with whom we are interacting?**

In 1990 a reporter from OMNI magazine traveled to Brazil to interview Paulo Freire for a feature article. The reporter, upon meeting Freire, engaged in the usual social banter preparatory to the formal interview. Soon he was ready to begin and moved to press the record button on his tape recorder. Before he reached the tape recorder, Freire placed his hand over the controls preventing the machine from being started.

"Before you turn that thing on, I want to talk to you," Freire said. "Tell me about your universe."

The reporter, a little taken aback, offered further conversation. He began safely with information about the magazine's readership circulation and the like. "Yes," Freire said, "Now tell me who you are." The reporter ventured a little deeper. When Freire got more excited, he would move to the edge of his chair, touch the reporter's knee, tap his hand, and generally claim his attention. The two were getting to know each other, establishing a relationship. They would now be able to have a much different conversation.

Freire understood that working with people is a matter of relationships. To establish relationships it is necessary to share a part of one's self. The more of one's self that is shared the more one relates to others as human beings. We must search for and claim every opportunity to establish relationships, for it is only upon deeper, positive relationships that learning will prosper. This is especially the case with young people for whom life presents a particular challenge. **What moral considerations should "adults in authority" require in our relationships with young people?**

---

❧ I SIT IN MY DESERTED CLASSROOM, exhausted with echoes of the day's activities lingering in the stillness. At 9 p.m., writing doesn't come easily or coherently for me, but as I sat down I knew I was going to write about Bobby, one of my students. I find my relationship with Bobby particularly rewarding because he is a student with whom other teachers have struggled. We came together first through our common love of NFL football. His favorite team was the Dallas Cowboys and mine was the Green Bay Packers and we often had vehement and emotional debates about upcoming games and the top players. Soon it became habitual for us to spend time together on Fridays to talk about the Sunday games (perhaps make some friendly wagers!) and to recap the weekend on Monday mornings. Eventually our relationship expanded into one in which we valued each other's support and company, beyond that of a traditional student–teacher relationship.

When Bobby was ill over the Christmas holidays and missed the first week of school in January, I remember sitting in the learning community Relaxation Zone in the mornings, drinking coffee, talking with kids, and actually missing Bobby's constant chatter. The morning of his return, he burst into the Relaxation Zone, stopped, looked at the students and teachers visiting, and frankly stated, "There's a lot of love in this room." We all shook our heads, laughed, and welcomed him back. Immediately, Bobby and I were entrenched in conversation about Christmas, family, football, and the disgusting details of his bout with the flu.

Today, as I pulled into the parking lot, I saw Bobby in the school doorway awaiting my arrival. He raced out to my car and lambasted me with questions about the learning community activity day. "Have you filled out the off-campus form for the ski trip?" "What time are the buses coming for the Leisure Center?" "Do you have attendance lists for the different activities?" He knew me well enough to know I wasn't a detail person and might not have everything in order. He proceeded to help me get everything organized. Later that day, I sat in the ski lodge with a group of about ten boys who were gossiping about who was dating whom in the learning community. I asked them which girls, if they had their choice, would they most like to go out with. This began a flurry of conversation, which Bobby briefly interrupted when he asked, "Other than you, Miss Morgan"? I love that kid.

Why was this an important story for Ms. Morgan? Why did she feel compelled to write the story? What makes relationships with students important for us? What makes Ms. Morgan's relationship with Bobby "rewarding"?

## Personalized School Environments

Teachers who work in personalized school environments rate relationships with students as one of the most satisfying aspects of their teaching. It increases their sense of professional efficacy.

"Despite the enormous demands on their time and energy, teachers in these environments stress their sense of satisfaction and professional pride.... Teachers speak of being challenged and of feeling valued as professionals and as human beings" (McLaughlin & Talbert, 1990, p. 232). This seems to describe the way Ms. Morgan values her relationship with Bobby.

What about the students' perspective? In a 1989 survey sponsored by the Girl Scouts of the United States of America, 7% of students said they would go to a teacher for advice and only one third said that their teachers cared for them. The percentage declines as students get older (Noddings, 1992). Is it important that our students feel we care for them and come to us for advice? McLaughlin and Talbert's (1990) study of personalized school environments found that "personal bonds with adults in the school have a greater capacity to motivate and engage than do traditional forms of social control . . . " (p. 230). Would Ms. Morgan have been able to engage Bobby in the planning of the ski trip had she not developed a personal bond with him? Bobby was described in the story as a student with whom other teachers had difficulties. Perhaps they never tried to get to know and understand him. Often it is a lack of connection and feelings of anonymity that cause students to disengage from school. Teachers wonder why some students are inattentive, uninterested, or simply absent. Perhaps these students feel invisible and unheard in our schools. Quite possibly we could engage these students if we recognized and valued each one as an individual.

Bobby and Ms. Morgan felt connected personally. Through recognizing one another as individuals and by providing support, many more students and teachers might enjoy a richer life in school. When we have places like the Relaxation Zone in which caring, support, and relationships are the focus, then we begin to break down some traditional educational barriers. When we recognize students as individuals with different needs, then we may question our traditional approach of enforcing the same rules for all students in the same way. Our sense of authority changes. It tends to be based on personal student-teacher relationships and individual responsibility instead of rules. This type of authority blurs the boundaries between the roles of students and teachers and begins to break down the traditional hierarchy. **To what extent could a personalized school environment break down the distinction between the institutionalized world of school and the outside world of friends, family, and social life?**

## Teacher as Friend

The students in the three schools with personalized environments studied by McLaughlin and Talbert (1990) said they "loved school" and repeatedly compared their schools to a family. Students claimed that the key to their success was the personal, individual recognition, and support they receive from the teachers. Valuing the role of family and friendship seems to play a large part in motivating and engaging students in school. Should teachers become friends with students? Paley (1979), in her work with primary children, argues the following:

> From the often negative function of judge and jury, the teacher can rise to the far more satisfying and useful position of friend. Strangers hide feelings and pretend to be what they are not. Friends want to know and talk about everything. It is a good environment in which to learn. (p. xv)

We recognize that people have many types of friendships with different people in their lives. Although these relationships are all quite different, they would have similar qualities, such as trust, open communication, honesty, care, and understanding. Is this the kind of friendship that Bobby and Ms. Morgan share? Could these qualities, then, describe a friendship between a teacher and a student?

❧ IT WAS HALLOWEEN and I felt as if my students had actually turned into the monsters they were dressed to be. We were in the middle of a hectic day of touring rooms to view costumes, a school assembly, and a wind-up class party. Much sugar had been consumed. The day's events had been taking their toll on me. Then Joel approached me. He had been transferred from another classroom due to behavior difficulties and an apparent personality conflict with the teacher. According to all accounts he was an unfocussed, disruptive, "bad" kid. I'd been working with him for three weeks and had learned to like him. But at this time of chaos, I fell prey to the talk of his reputation. He quietly approached me and asked, "Miss Garfunkel?" Wondering what he could have done to make him so sheepish, I snapped, "What Joel?"

Placing his hand on my knee, he said, "You look so sad, do you want some of my candy?" I was touched. Of all the students, Joel was the only one at that time who looked beyond his own needs to perceive mine. Later I wondered, "Who is Joel anyway?" The mere mention of his name conjured up an image which had been developed by staff-room talk over the course of two years. Does this mean that he had to be this person to me? The Joel of the staff-room talk wouldn't have been the perceptive, caring boy who offered me his candy. I realized that Joel deserved a fresh start, just as all of us do at some points in our lives. It is quite possible that Joel and I had given each other fresh starts.

Joel is more than a student. He is first and above all a person, a young human being. He is a person who has struggled with life and a student with whom teachers have struggled. But how is Joel defined? Our response is fundamental to Joel's learning. If Joel's struggles are with his world outside of school—his family, relations, friends, and so on—then he is surely not going to shelve these trials, clear his mind, and buckle down to learning things that are likely quite unrelated to his life. Few youngsters do this easily. Troubled youngsters have considerable difficulty.

## Defining Young People

If young people like Joel are defined as "students" within the context of traditional school and classroom conventions, then that role, i.e., student, may not fully recognize their humanity. Perhaps young people need to be recognized as already possessing knowledge and already having ways of presenting themselves to the world. **In what ways do we acknowledge and value the life experiences of young people as fundamental toward their becoming more capable and caring human beings?**

≈ MY BROTHER, PETER, is four years younger than I am. Until he started college a few years ago, he disliked school. I wonder, as an educator, what causes young people to "turn off" school so early in life. For my brother, it began in fourth grade. During that school year Peter's teacher, Mrs. Graham, decided that he needed extra help in reading. She arranged for him to go to a learning assistance center (LAC) two mornings a week. Peter had to leave his regular class in the mid-morning and make his way to the LAC class by way of public transit. No one else from his class was attending the LAC so he had to travel alone. I remember how upset he was about having to go at all and about having to travel alone. My Mom made arrangements, through an understanding boss, to leave her office to take Peter to and from his LAC classes. For the few months that Peter attended LAC his feelings about it ranged from sadness to anger to powerlessness, and worst of all, to shame. Peter was only in the LAC classes for a short time before they deemed him ready to be back in his regular classroom. But by then the damage had been done. He believed he was "dumb."

Peter achieved borderline passing grades until his senior year, during which he was lucky enough to have a number of teachers who believed in him and his abilities. They encouraged him to study hard so that he could go to college. Soon Peter began to believe he could do well . . . and he did. Now he is in his third year of college, earning honors grades in sociology.

He and I talked recently about our school experiences and his LAC experience was mentioned. These were his reactions: "I'm still trying to repress that you know." "Luckily, I had some good friends who didn't make fun of me, or it could have been even worse." "It did me more harm than good." "It was one of the worst experiences of my life." After our conversation, I knew I needed to write this story.

Most likely, Mrs. Graham thought she was doing what was best for Peter. He wasn't up to grade level in reading so something had to be done. The school system was organized in such a way that these separate learning centers managed students with learning difficulties. The LAC, for Mrs. Graham, was a convenient and acceptable way of managing Peter's reading problem. Today, sending students to separate centers or schools to "remediate" problems is not so prevalent. Instead, young people struggling with their academic learning are often sent to separate classrooms for periods of time. Would this arrangement have had an effect on Peter similar to that of the LAC? The elimination of travel to the LAC may have softened the blow, but it would have been a blow nonetheless. Peter would still have felt segregated from his classmates. He would still have been labeled a "slow learner" and most likely would have gone on to believe that he was dumb.

It seems that the organizational structures many schools have in place tend to manage, quite conveniently and neatly, the students labeled with learning difficulties. However, the managing and labeling of young people has detrimental effects, as Peter's story tells. Young people defined by these bureaucratically bestowed labels feel stripped of their individuality and their humanness.

Imagine Mrs. Graham's response to Peter if she had understood and valued him as an equal human being? Her new perspective would not have made his reading level magically rise, but it certainly would have affected how Peter felt about school and about himself. Mrs. Graham would not have seen a student with a "reading problem," but a young person with talents, strengths as well as weaknesses, interests, and feelings. When students are defined in this way, as human beings, the need or desire for labels disappears. Perhaps Mrs. Graham could have tapped Peter's vivid imagination to help him achieve in reading. Through an understanding of Peter, she may have been able to find some reading material of particular interest to him. In any case, the caring emanating from her understanding of his humanness would likely have rendered the LAC option unacceptable.

Peter's voice echoing, "It was one of the worst experiences of my life," demands that educators explore alternatives to labeling and excluding young people from our classrooms. The discussion of Peter brings to mind the voices of people in previous stories. We hear Anne asking, "Why do we have to learn this stuff anyway?" We remember Debbie and Andrea's exuberant fund-raising, envision Ms. Morgan and Bobby animatedly talking about football, and see "bad kid" Joel trying to comfort Miss Garfunkel. The stories raise compelling questions about how we define young people.

1. To what extent do we respect and understand young people as human beings?

2. Do our learning environments offer a moral context that promotes personal ownership?

3. How do we provide opportunities to experience authentic responsibility?

4. How do we understand teachers and students as co-learners within the context of the social construction of knowledge and meaning?

5. Are young people provided with an active voice in decisions about learning and life?

6. To what extent do we give young people control over learning choices, to satisfy the need for intrinsic motivation?

7. How do we understand and take into consideration the importance of the young person's intention?

Through these ways of defining young people our responses to learning would assume a different complexion. Levin (1992) reminds us, "The way you define children has an awful lot to do with the way you work with them" (p. 20). But lists, questions, and exhortations alone will not cause changes in the ways people are defined. Only personal reflection and profound questioning of deeply held beliefs will challenge the assumptions that drive practice.

## AN INVITATION TO THE READER

The following page suggests a process for thinking about the chapter, to stimulate conversation, encourage debate, share stories, provoke further questions, challenge current thinking, or engage in further personal reflection. University classes, professional development groups, school staffs, and parent groups may find the chapter's questions and related text useful, as a challenge to personal beliefs, understandings and experiences, toward affirmation or change.

We present the concept of "filter." Readers are invited to consider the central question of the chapter, along with the questions that arise from the text. It is not our intention to limit or reduce context to one small portion of the chapter—we are conscious of the problem of reductionism. It is our hope that, as readers proceed through the book, they will respond to questions in a more holistic manner.

The concept of filter is a metaphor for the reader's personal beliefs, values, and experiences, through which new ideas are explored and current beliefs challenged. It is this filtering that provides an opportunity for the reader to make personal connections to the questions and ideas in the chapter. This process may provide an opportunity to deepen meaning and understanding of the concepts and ideas discussed.

**In the following framework, you are invited to contemplate your beliefs, understandings, and experiences through reflecting on the questions and related text in Chapter 3.**

**TO WHAT EXTENT ARE LEARNERS RECOGNIZED AS COMPLETE HUMAN BEINGS?**
Central organizing question for Chapter 3

How might teachers invite learning in ways that respect the humanness of the learner?
Text reference: Page 49.
Related discussion: Pages 43–59.

How are young people defined and treated in schools?
Text reference: Page 49.
Related discussion: Pages 49–59.

How often do we dismiss young people when they appeal to our interest?
Text reference: Page 51.
Related discussion: Pages 51–56.

In what ways do organizational arrangements, teaching methods, and facility use prevent young people from sharing dreams and, more important, prevent teachers from establishing relationships that encourage mutual responses?
Text reference: Page 51.
Related discussion: Pages 49–55.

How do we create conditions where relationships develop, where young people are respected as human beings, where intervention into lives is mutual, and where dreams are shared?
Text reference: Page 52.
Related discussion: Pages 51–55.

How can we engage in productive interaction without understanding the person or persons with whom we are interacting?
Text reference: Page 52.
Related discussion: Pages 52–59.

What moral consideration, should 'adults in authority' require in our relationships with young people?
Text reference: Page 53.
Related discussion: Pages 52–59.

To what extent could a personalized school environment break down the distinction between the institutionalized world of school and the outside world of friends, family, and social life?
Text reference: Page 55.
Related discussion: Pages 54–59.

In what ways do we acknowledge and value the life experiences of young people as fundamental toward their becoming more capable and caring human beings?
Text reference: Page 56.
Related discussion: Pages 52–59.

**Filter of personal beliefs, understandings, and experiences**

*Personal journal*

# REFERENCES

Aoki, T. (1991). *Inspiriting the curriculum and pedagogy: Talks to teachers*. Edmonton, Alberta: University of Alberta Press.

Levin, H. (1992, September). On building learning communities: A conversation with Hank Levin. *Educational Leadership, 50*(1), 19–23.

McLaughlin, M., & Talbert, J. (1990, November). Constructing a personalized school environment. *Phi Delta Kappan, 72*(3), 230–235.

Noddings, N. (1992). *The challenge of care in schools*. New York: Teachers' College Press.

Paley, V. (1979). *White teacher*. Cambridge, MA: Harvard University Press.

# SUGGESTED READINGS

Two articles by NEL NODDINGS (1995, January, May) provide further elaboration on the matter of caring. "Teaching Themes of Care," in *Phi Delta Kappan 76*(9), 675–679, presents a strong case that caring and developing people who care is fundamental in teaching. She urges teachers and parents to show their caring by cooperating in children's activities. In a second article, "A Morally Defensible Mission for Schools in the 21st Century," *Phi Delta Kappan 76*(5), 365–368, she takes the position that the main educational aim for schools should be to encourage the growth of competent, caring, loving, and lovable people. Schools as agents of society need to care for children, reduce violence, respect work of every kind, reward excellence, and ensure a place for every child and emerging adult in the economic and social world.

A book by LEE BOLMAN and TERRENCE DEAL (1995), though not focused on schooling, should provide an interesting supplement to this chapter. *Leading with Soul: An Uncommon Journey of Spirit* (San Francisco: Jossey-Bass) takes the form of a story in which a beleaguered executive searches for passion and purpose in work and life. The book argues that the work place needs a language of moral discourse that permits discussions of ethical and spiritual issues, connecting them to concepts of management and leadership. We believe the message of this book complements an essential aspect of Chapter 3, respecting and responding to young people as human beings. The question we posed, **"How do we create the conditions where relationships develop, where young people are respected as human beings, where intervention into lives is mutual, and where dreams are shared?"** would be informed by this book.

JULIAN WEISSGLASS (1996, April) explores the social transformations necessary to change schools into institutions that completely respect young people. "Transforming Schools into Caring Learning Communities," *Journal for a Just and Caring Education*, 2(2), 175–189 presents methods that have been successfully used to improve teachers' listening skills and address fundamental issues surrounding trust, confidence, active engagement, self-acceptance, equity, and emotional well-being.

# 4

# LEARNING AND LIFE

## AN INVITATION . . .

Chapter 4 invites the reader to consider the degree to which in-school learning is connected to life. The chapter begins with the position that the traditional view of learning is governed by the teacher in the role of gatekeeper of knowledge. Required subjects tend to be presented in fragmented, unconnected ways, with little connection to lived experiences.

**To what extent are the ways we ask young people to learn appropriate for today's complex and changing world?**

In any learning endeavor, opportunities to rehearse and apply learning to meaningful contexts is vital. Young people come to school to learn, and their learning should help them understand and deal with life. This chapter discusses the need for our learning focus to move toward involving young people in posing problems, investigating along with the teacher, constructing understanding and making meaning, doing, performing, demonstrating, and generally experiencing learning with choice, voice, and humanness. The chapter concludes with a recognition of the immediacy of life for young people and that learning should, to a considerable extent, connect directly to their lives and build on previous experiences.

❧ ❧ ❧

 WE GATHERED EVERYONE AROUND A TABLE in the library. Each core subject-area teacher, the fine-arts and practical-arts teachers, the counselor, and the administration all sat to discuss Billy's poor performance on the latest report card. Billy was disruptive and performing below grade level in math. He had managed to scrape through in science and was doing reasonably well in humanities. He even showed some strength in his fine arts options.

"Billy is a pain," one teacher said. "He never pays attention and he does not do any homework."

"He needs extra help in math because his skills are so low," the math teacher explained.

As the dialogue continued, it became clear that we needed to make some adjustments and so did Billy. The decision was made to pull Billy out of one of his fine-arts options and replace it with a remedial help course. We hoped that it would benefit Billy and set him up for success.

Clearly, the teachers in the story are truly interested in helping Billy. They hoped that the extra remedial help class would benefit Billy and set him up for success. However, the question that needs to be posed is: Will taking Billy out of a class in which he is showing strength and put him in one that gives him more of what he is weak at, lead to greater success? Give Billy more of what he is not good at seems to be the solution. If he gets more time to practice his math skills then he is sure to improve his grade. Does this seem like a reasonable assumption?

# CHALLENGING WAYS OF LEARNING

Educators often equate the amount of time spent on a particular subject with the amount of learning that takes place. If a student like Billy spends two hours a day on math, instead of one hour, then, ipso facto, he will learn more math. It seems as though the teachers in the story have neglected to honestly examine themselves and their teaching. In other words, the teachers believe they and their teaching methods are fine, but Billy is not. Do these teachers view learning as the simple acquisition of knowledge and Billy as a passive recipient of instruction? Is it possible that the teachers in the story need to question the ways in which they organize for learning? Should they question the ways in which they are asking young people to learn? In looking for answers, the teachers could consider the following ideas and theories:

- multiple intelligences
- managed learning
- student voice and choice
- relevance and connectedness
- authenticity and the process of becoming
- teacher as expert
- teacher as co-learner
- independence and empowerment
- personalized learning
- rehearsal and application
- negotiation and voice

## Multiple Intelligences

Gardner (1993) promotes the theory of multiple intelligences. His theory holds that all students are intelligent to varying degrees in a number of intelligences: linguistic, musical, logical–mathematical, spatial, bodily–kinesthetic, interpersonal, and intrapersonal. Billy's good performance in his fine arts options appears to show a strength in the intelligences defined by Gardner as musical and spatial. However, according to his grades in math and science, Billy appears to be experiencing difficulty in the logical–mathematical domain. Although the teachers in the story did not question their teaching, Gardner claims that, "with good teaching, individuals can develop, can actually get smarter, in each of these seven intelligences." (In Black, 1994, p. 24) The extra math class may enhance Billy's intelligence in the mathematical domain, but Billy's removal from the fine arts may, in fact, deny Billy the opportunity to discover his intelligence of "promise," his real passion. Black (1994) points out that, "once students leave school, how far will mathematical and linguistic skills take them? How many careers or other endeavors, such as serious hobbies or avocations, depend on the knowledge a person gains from spending twelve years in school?" (p. 26) **What would be the implications for curriculum if teachers were to consider the intelligences of students in the design of learning opportunities?**

---

❧ I TOOK A UNIVERSITY COURSE with a teacher, Sonia Connors, who told a compelling story about a young girl named Lynn in her third-grade class.

Lynn loved to draw. In fact she wanted to spend most of her school day drawing. Sonia could persuade Lynn to work on math and reading, but when it came to putting pen to paper to write, all that pen seemed to do was draw. At first Sonia tried to pry Lynn away from drawing to work on her writing skills. Lynn stubbornly refused.

Tired of these power struggles, Sonia reflected on her actions and wondered if Lynn could use her drawing to learn to write. The next day, when Sonia asked the class to write a story, she saw Lynn pull out her pencil crayons and begin to draw. This time, when Sonia approached, she did not get into the usual battle with putting away the art and getting out the writing. Instead, she asked if Lynn would draw her story first then write about what she had drawn. Lynn, surprised but happy, drew her picture. Sonia continued this approach and soon Lynn became a more confident writer and her stories became longer and more elaborate.

---

Sonia and Billy's teachers had similar concerns about their students. Both Lynn and Billy were having difficulties in certain domains. Sonia, however, sought out a different approach, one that respected Lynn's passion for drawing, but also helped her experience some success in writing. Sonia recognized the need for attention to humanness in learning.

A more likely response in schools today would have been to react as Billy's teachers did: Decrease the amount of drawing Lynn was allowed to do and ask her to work solely on her writing skills. This common response is akin to the mental models (Senge, 1990) discussed in Chapter 2. These taken-for-granted beliefs, many of which may be subconscious, tend to limit our thinking. The teachers' mental models would continue to inspire and influence their attitude, understanding and behavior toward conventional practices, until their deeply held beliefs and assumptions could be brought to the surface for challenge. Here lies a key difference between Sonia and Billy's teachers. While Billy's teachers acted within the boundaries of their mental models, Sonia stopped to reflect on her responses. She questioned her previous actions and was able to re-story her work with Lynn in quite an unconventional way.

The powerful role of assumptions and mindscapes is worthy of attention, as we consider the effectiveness of learning in our schools. The unchallenged assumptions, which drive a teacher's responses to the learning needs of young people, may well lead, as illustrated in Billy's story, to a learning environment that adheres to the tradition and glue of social convention, in ways that constrain and impede effective learning. However, Lynn's story shows the promise that the challenging of assumptions holds.

## Managed Learning

The origins of contemporary schooling, discussed in Chapter 1, are well documented. The scientific principles espoused by Taylor (1911) provided methods of advanced production to industrial and manufacturing establishments. In his zeal, Taylor was convinced that the same principles could "be applied with equal force to all social activities" (p. 157). In this regard he included the management of homes, farms, large and small businesses, churches, institutions, universities, and government departments.

During its infancy, schooling was an impressionable institution, markedly influenced by the technical–rational dogma of the times. As "advanced production methods" were applied, classrooms became stops on the assembly line of knowledge. Work became fragmented and teachers neatly compartmentalized learning.

THE BELL RANG and the students began to file into Mr. Bono's class. One by one they sat down in their designated row, looked up at Mr. Bono, and awaited instruction. The lesson began with the students taking out their note books and copying down some notes from the blackboard. Mr. Bono then began to discuss four types of thermometers and how they measure heat. A couple of students asked questions and then a series of textbook questions were assigned.

Peter seemed to be off task. He was looking around the room, glancing at the text on occasion. Peter then turned around and asked Joe a question. All of a sudden Mr. Bono spoke, "Please turn around Peter; if you need some help put up your hand and I will come to help you." Before long the class was over.

If our story is at all representative of today's classrooms, there is little doubt that the industrial model is alive and well in schools. However, in this age of information and service we must honestly question the appropriateness of the ways we are asking young people to learn. Let us place ourselves into the story with Mr. Bono to uncover the mental models that describe our attitudes toward learning, teaching, and school organization. Let us consider in a general way some common school practices, listed in Figure 4.1, brought to light by the story and the assumptions that drive them. Are the assumptions congruent with current knowledge about learning?

Of course, these activities and assumptions are generalized from our story. There are many instances in schools where informed and enlightened approaches to learning provide powerful experiences for young people. The generalized examples are, however, offered here as both typical and provocative, with the intention of stimulating thought. It might also be useful for the reader to refer to the questions posed in Chapter 3 about the humanness of the learner. In the spirit of reflection and after the advice of Senge (1990), we invite you to "tell the truth about current reality" (p. 54), as only the truth will expose any incongruency between practice and contemporary knowledge. The reason we do things the way we do in schools can no longer be based on an incessant need to "manage" learning. We must continually look to the future and ask ourselves about the appropriateness of the ways we ask young people to learn for our complex and changing world.

| Learning Activity | Assumption |
|---|---|
| Whole-group learning | The whole class will be interested in and learn from the oral presentation. |
| Teacher-directed learning | The teacher should determine the necessary knowledge for the students to acquire. |
| Students engage in independent seat work | Student collaboration is not necessary for successful learning. |
| All students work on the same text questions | All students are at the same level of understanding and learning. |
| Science as a specialized discipline | Each subject is an entity to itself and should be taught as such. |
| Students may raise their hands if they wish to ask any questions about their class assignment. | The teacher controls all learning. The teacher provides permission to speak. |

**FIGURE 4.1**
Common School Practices and Assumptions

👈 IT WAS A TYPICAL TUESDAY MORNING—team meeting day. The six of us gathered around a table, enjoyed some doughnuts, and sipped our coffee. It was a great way to ease ourselves into the morning's discussion: What skills, attributes, and competencies are important for our young people to develop? This was the question that was to guide our conversation. We began by sharing an employability skills document, curriculum guides, and our personal stories, experiences, knowledge, and philosophies as educators. We developed five categories and under each we outlined specific skills and competencies we would like to see developed in our students. They included academic, social, and personal development. The conversation was rich and we were excited about the ideas we were generating.

Then, a tough question was asked: How might we see student development demonstrated? Could we find out if our students had improved in the social, personal, and academic ways we had hoped? We began to talk about how students could play an important role in their own learning and assessment. One person suggested that students should decide on a topic and make a presentation, which would demonstrate their understanding. The brainstorm was on! We came up with what we called OPPs, or Open Personal Projects, named after the No. 1 rap song of the time. Students, individually or in groups, would outline a topic or issue they were most interested in researching and to which they would apply their skills and competencies. This way students were able to determine what connections they could make between the skills and competencies and their own lives, and teachers were comfortable that well defined goals were being striven for.

What was it about the OPP idea that these teachers found so compelling? Why did allowing students to choose an issue in which they were interested make sense? Perhaps we need to look at some beliefs about learning and knowledge that may underlie the teachers' conversation.

## Student Voice and Choice

"Each of us makes sense of our world by synthesizing new experiences into what we have previously come to understand" (Brooks & Brooks, 1993, p. 4). This is a belief about knowledge from a constructivist point of view, which connects to the conversation described in the story. The teachers were striving to find a way for students to connect the new skills and competencies to their previous understandings and experiences. They hoped that the OPPs would provide such a context for learning. Current research tends to support the view that human beings produce, share, and transform knowledge as individuals and as groups (Leinhardt, 1992). This also seems to be an underlying belief of the teachers in the story who recognized their students as producers, sharers, and transformers of knowledge. In recognizing young people as active knowledge constructors, teachers, in turn, must invite students to ask their own questions and seek their own answers. For the teachers in the story the invitation came in the form of the Open Personal Project. Invitations such as these offer choices to students. What question is more important? How will I seek out solutions? Who will I need to help me? How can I present my work?

Why would being empowered to ask themselves such questions be valuable for young people? The benefits of self-determination and choice for students are compelling. First, for psychological, emotional, and even physical well being, it is important for people to experience a sense of control in their lives. In fact, few things lead to depression more quickly than a feeling of powerlessness (Kohn, 1993). How often do students feel helpless or powerless in schools? Second, the development of responsibility, decision-making skills, and a greater understanding of what kind of people they want to be, occurs only when students are provided with opportunities to live out authentic experiences. "We cannot expect children to accept ready-made values and truths all the way through school, and then suddenly make choices in adulthood" (Kohn, 1993). A third benefit of providing opportunities for choice is evidence of increased standardized test results, creativity, pride in work, reasoning skills, and motivation. Finally, and most important, allowing young people, as human beings, to make decisions about their own lives is preferable to controlling them. Is it possible that these benefits of choice in learning may be lived out as the students construct their OPPs?

To this point we have been trying to make sense of the underlying beliefs and understandings of the teachers in the story. Now we would like to turn to the students. What might their response be? Smith and Johnson (1993) worked with a seventh grade language arts teacher to provide a learning environment that valued adolescent voices. Here are some quotes from the students' journals:

> If the outlook of the subject is more interesting to the student . . . the more the student is going to want to learn (Len, p. 18).
>
> We should make the decisions about what we learn in class. After all, we're the ones who have to sit in school all day. So, in a nutshell, we should be able to choose, within a limit, what we want to learn (B.J., p. 18).
>
> I am an okay learner. I think I could work a little better if my teachers would just **move over a little** [emphasis by the authors]. I can do more work if I can do it myself (Stacy, p. 18).

Young people desire and need to feel their voices are heard and valued. They want to have a sense of ownership of their learning, to be included in decisions, to have teachers "move over" and work in a collaborative relationship with them. Our story continues with students exploring their OPP issues and the teachers learning to "move over a little":

---

FOR THE FIRST OPP some of the skills that needed to be demonstrated were an application of the scientific method, designing different types of graphs, percent calculations, research skills, paragraph writing, and conducting an interview. Socially and personally, we hoped students would make reasoned decisions, take responsibility for their learning, self-evaluate, and care for and communicate with people in their group. In the two-week period the students were to research their topic, and create a written, visual, and oral presentation. The form that each of these took was to be determined by the students. We hoped this would allow the individual students to tap their unique gifts, talents, and creativity.

Many of the topics chosen were surprisingly academic: the abortion issue, China, the destruction of the rain forest, and famous artists. However, my team-teaching partner, Jim, and I were concerned about two groups in the class. We wondered if they would be able to take ownership of their projects and work well in this less-structured two weeks. One was a group of four girls whose topic was "Makeup For Teens in the '90s" and the other group was five boys who were working together on "Nintendo." But one of the major reasons we were doing OPPs with our students was that we believed that if students had a voice in their curriculum at school and brought their interests into academia they would be more motivated to learn. So we did our best to facilitate successful research for all the students, constantly reminding them not to forget the skills they had to apply, but trying not to undermine their leadership and choice during the OPP. The students had the opportunity to go on self-directed off-campus research trips, with parental permission, to locations they thought relevant to their topic. Most of the groups went to museums, public libraries, hospitals, abortion clinics, churches, and cultural centers. The makeup group went to the mall. The Nintendo group went to the video arcade and toy store in the area. Jim and I continued to worry.

On OPP demonstration and presentation day, excitement and pride was in the air. All students toured the learning community to look at the projects of the others and share their own. Then came time for the oral and visual presentations to the class. All the presentations were unique and valued by the class—even Ralph Randolph's project on gophers. The students studying the rain forest had shocking statistics, beautiful illustrations, and an informative skit involving loggers and environmentalists. The group looking at the issue of abortion organized a class debate. We learned about different cultures, how to say a few words in other languages, the backgrounds of famous actors, and many other things that interested the students. Jim and I anxiously awaited the makeup and Nintendo presentations.

The amount of work and effort demonstrated in the presentations surprised us. These students who were generally hard to motivate did extensive and beautiful work on their OPPs. The Nintendo boys had graph after graph of data on games, memory, cost, graphics, and sound systems. They surveyed our students on how much of their free time they spent playing Nintendo, watching television, talking on the phone, hanging out with friends, and doing homework. This was a real eye opener for many of us.

The girls studying makeup did an incredible job, too. They had graphs of price comparisons, longest-wearing lipsticks, waterproof mascaras, and smudge-proof eyeliners. They surveyed other eighth-grade girls about what type of makeup they wore, and why they wore makeup. They raised the issue of trying to look like the young women in magazines and recommended to the girls not to get caught up in the potential danger of anorexia or poor self-esteem. Makeovers were done to four students in front of the class. This was fun for the participants as well as the observers, especially when Albert Nogales volunteered to be made over.

Our first attempt at OPPs was successful enough for us to continue with them at different points in the year and reaffirmed our belief that when student voice is heard and plays an important role in curriculum, young people are motivated to learn.

---

As the teachers "moved over," the students flourished with a greater sense of responsibility and personal control.

## Relevance and Connectedness

The young people were able to connect academic skills to OPP topics that emanated from their own life experiences and knowledge. They were able to design appropriate learning tasks and make reasonable decisions. The value of process was learned as they demonstrated acquired skills and knowledge. Provided with rights and privileges, the students learned responsibility. They began to exercise their voice and in it we heard their social and personal concerns intertwined with the academic work. We believe that as teachers, "we attempt to acknowledge our students as collaborators in the learning cycle. We remember that they, too, have agendas, knowledge, needs, and desires to learn information that is relevant to their lives and topics under study." (Smith & Johnson, 1993, pg. 29) **In what ways could educators build collaborative relationships with students?** How do we learn to "move over"? Duckworth (1987) would consider the recognizing of the "wonderful ideas" of young people to be a part of moving over. She believes that providing opportunities and facilitating experiences for students to have occasion for their own wonderful ideas and feel good about having them, is the essence of pedagogy. She tells the following story of a student called Hank:

Hank was an energetic and not very scholarly fifth grader. His class had been learning about electric circuits with flashlight batteries, bulbs, and various wires. After the children had developed considerable familiarity with these materials, the teacher made a number of mystery boxes. Two wires protruded from each box, but inside, unseen, each box had a different way of making contact between the wires. In one box the wires were attached to a battery; in another they were attached to a bulb; in a third, to a certain length of resistance wire; in a fourth box they were not attached at all; and so forth. By trying to complete the circuit on the outside of a box, the children were able to figure out what made the connection inside the box. Like many other children, Hank attached a battery and a bulb to the wire outside the box. Because the bulb lit, he knew at least that the wires inside the box were connected in some way. But, because it was somewhat dimmer than usual, he also knew that the wires inside were not connected directly to each other and that they were not connected by a piece of ordinary copper wire. Along with many of the children, he knew that the degree of dimness of the bulb meant that the wires inside were connected either by another bulb of the same kind or by a certain length of resistance wire.

The teacher expected them to go only this far. However, to push the children to think a little further, she asked them if they could tell whether it was a bulb or a piece of wire inside the box. She herself thought there was no way to tell. After some thought, Hank had an idea. He undid the battery and bulb that he had already attached on the outside of the box. In their place, using additional copper wire, he attached six batteries in a series. He had already experimented enough to know that six batteries would burn out a bulb, if it was a bulb inside the box. He also knew that once a bulb is burned out, it no longer completes the circuit. He then attached the original battery and bulb again. This time the bulb on the outside of the box did not light. So he reasoned, rightly, that there had been a bulb inside the box and that now it was burned out. If there had been a wire inside, it would not have burned through and the bulb on the outside would still light (pp. 6–7). *Excerpt as submitted from* Piaget in the Classroom *by Milton Schwebel and Jane Raph. © 1973 by Basic-Books, Inc. Reprinted by permission of BasicBooks, a division of HarperCollins Publishers, Inc.*

Duckworth urges teachers to provide settings that suggest wonderful ideas to children; settings that access a child's reality and respect their individuality. She posits that the more children experience wonderful ideas and enjoy their intellectual challenge, "the more likely it is that they will some day happen upon wonderful ideas that no one else has happened upon before" (p. 7). Such experiences and opportunities require teachers to risk sharing control and power, trying new ideas, and moving in different directions. Perhaps teachers, too, need to feel confident about their own wonderful ideas, so that they might feel free to be co-learners with young people. If teachers like Jim and his partner in the OPP story, are to accept the imagination, divergence, and creativity of their students, then they must be willing to risk change in themselves and in the nature of their classrooms. This type of change is described by Green (1986):

> Somehow, we who are teachers and inquirers, we who love children, have to try—with their help—to read the world as it presents itself to them. We realize that, for us as well as for the children, to live is to experience a situation in terms of its meanings; and the best we can do is try to uncover, to come clear. . . . No longer taking the stance of outside observer, or anatomist, or quantifier, we can engage with children in a quest for what is possible. We can beckon; we can urge; we can sustain them when they break from anchorage, so long as we are willing to break from anchorage ourselves (p. 783).

The story that follows explores the relationship of a teacher and a young woman in his class as she "breaks from anchorage":

᥊ KATHY'S CLASS WAS IN THE MIDDLE of their ninth-grade year and their social studies class was providing opportunities to learn in different ways. The teacher, Mr. Russell, had established three broad learning choices. The first kind was structured: Nearly all the time was to be spent with the teacher. The second kind allowed for a balance between independent time and time with the teacher. The third kind was predominantly independent study.

Kathy was fairly typical for a teen-ager. She was strongly influenced by her peers, not highly organized, and easily distracted. Her sense of responsibility was not consistent with what her teacher considered reasonable. In Kathy's social studies class, young people were invited to reflect on themselves and to discuss with the teacher which kind of learning would be best for them. Kathy argued persuasively to learn in the predominantly independent mode. It was important in this particular experience that the young people learned about themselves.

Kathy's pattern was predictable. In spite of the regular conferences with the teacher she was not successful. At each conference she was asked questions that invited her to make judgments about herself. Each time she convinced herself that she could turn things around. Kathy fell flat on her face. She was desperately upset when the final results were declared, even though she had been party to the accumulation of marks throughout her learning experience. Should the teacher have allowed Kathy to assume so much control over her learning? Wouldn't it have been better, even more appropriate, for the teacher to have laid the law down and insisted, in Kathy's best interests, that she join the highly structured group? Would Kathy have learned more that way?

Some twenty years later Kathy met her teacher in a shopping mall quite by surprise. They had not seen each other in this time. During the conversation about old times, Kathy recalled the learning experience we have been discussing. Her remarks were telling. "Mr. Russell, I just have to tell you that it was because of you that I learned something about myself that really helped me to be successful in high school and probably beyond. You were the only person who let me take some control over my life and allowed me to come face-to-face with myself. All around me, people were telling me what to do and giving me so many opportunities to rebel. With you there was nothing to rebel against, only myself. You let me 'goof up,' but the most important thing was you helped me to pick myself up and I really learned from that."

A problem was posed for Kathy in this story. Mr. Russell allowed Kathy's problem to develop, so that she might work it through, to eventually make meaning for herself. For Freire (1988), in problem posing education, people "develop their power to perceive critically the way they exist in the world with which and in which they find themselves . . . [and] takes [humanity's] historicity as their starting point. Problem posing education affirms [people] as beings in the process of becoming. . . " (pp. 71–72).

## Authenticity and the Process of Becoming

Kathy was in the process of becoming. Had Mr. Russell not realized this and instead insisted that she join the structured group, she would have been denied an opportunity to learn about herself. This discovery, described poignantly by Kathy, was important in her process of becoming. Perhaps this is what school ought to be about, the finding that we ourselves are interesting. If young people are eager to learn about themselves and about their process of becoming, they need opportunities to make sense of the world in which they are becoming. In this light, educators would need to be concerned "not solely with development, but with children as moral agents, children as seekers, children struggling to orient themselves in an uncertain world" (Green, 1986, p. 776).

Is this how Mr. Russell perceived Kathy? As teachers begin to define young people in this way, it changes how they work and the type of relationships that develop in their classrooms. Mr. Russell recognized Kathy and, indeed, himself, in the process of becoming. This changed the way he organized his classes, units of study, and evaluation—allowing the process of becoming, no matter how painful, to be lived out.

Through these processes, teachers and students become partners and value one another's humanity. They seek to understand one another, teach one another, and learn about their ever-transforming world. Paley (1991) writes about her search to understand the children of her kindergarten.

"John, I want to ask you something." John and I are walking, hand in hand, to gymnasium. The reason we are holding hands has everything to do with the fact that John has been taking flying leaps up the walls of the corridor. "What do you want to ask?" he says suspiciously. "How come you like to play checkers so much but you won't play Battleship?" "My Daddy plays checkers," he says. "But, you know, checkers is really much harder. If you can play checkers as well as you do, Battleship will really be easy." "Naw, me and Daddy plays checkers. Then he lets me get on his back and then I start to fall and then he grabs me. He never lets me fall. And then he laughs."

"We could tell your Daddy how to play Battleship," I suggest. "Naw, he don't like that game." Then John looks at me kindly. "But if you need someone to play with you, I could play checkers soonest I get back, okay?" "Sure, let's do that. And then you can tell me again how to climb on your Daddy's back." I decide to forget about Battleship for a while, but after our checkers game I give it one more try. "John, were you there when I made that big mistake in the Battleship game?" He is interested in my mistakes. They all are. "What did you do?" "Come on, I'll show you." He comes quickly and so do a few others. I sketch out new grids and place them alongside the corrected ones. Then I proceed step by step through my error as if I am telling a story. John stares at the board but does not catch the point of my story. I can see that. Nonetheless, it is my mistake, not his, and so he stays.

Lilly tells him, "See, Mrs. Paley made this big mistake. She forgot to put all the ABCDE on top." John has lost interest in the board and is looking at me with the same look he gave me when I was on my way to the doctor. "Did you feel bad when you made the big mistake?" he asks me. "I really did, at first," I reply. John and I have begun to know and trust one another. We are no longer strangers. Everything good will flow from this fact.

What good things will flow? Will John learn to play Battleship, will he sit still at group time, and will he fill his folder with whatever I decide to collect? These are legitimate school concerns, but we must also ask: Will John continue to tell us his dreams and accept a role in ours? Can he smile when he enters the classroom and feel the expansiveness of being with family? Does John care about us and know that we care about him? Most important, does John care about himself, and know that a whole world is inside of himself worth investigating and developing? (pp. 165–166) *© 1991 by Kappa Delta Pi, an International Honor Society in Education. Reprinted by permission.*

As we read about John, we wondered about learning activities that would encourage young people to care about, discover, and develop themselves. We considered the roles of teachers and students within a classroom that valued this process of becoming: **What might a learning environment look like when a teacher tries to understand the role and feelings of students?** What implications might the learning assumptions shown in Figure 4.2 have for classroom practice?

| Learning Activity | Assumption | Implications for Practice |
|---|---|---|
| Students working in cooperative groups | Students will learn successfully from and with peers guided by knowledgeable, competent, and caring adults. | |
| Students working through a variety of learning strategies; some computing, some with the teacher, some in small groups, some in the library, and so on | Learning characterized by variety and flexibility responds more successfully to emerging needs and interests. | |
| Students posing questions and seeking answers | Students directing their learning will benefit from opportunities to negotiate meaning and context. | |
| Students having some genuine control over their learning and the opportunities to make their own choices | Power and control devolved to students produces greater commitment, ownership, and success. | |
| Students demonstrating learning in authentic ways | Authentic demonstrations of learning provide more accurate indicators of learning success. | |
| Student involvement in decisions about long-range learning plans in which life-related topics present core organizers | Learning planned with young people will be more meaningful for them; more connected to their lives. | |

**FIGURE 4.2**
Learning Assumptions

     I WALKED INTO THE BIG ROOM, where all six teachers' desks were located, during a math class that Arthur and Drew were team-teaching. I needed to retrieve an item from my file cabinet. My intention of dashing in and out quickly changed once I observed what was going on. I stayed for the entire class. The interaction between Arthur, Drew, and the students was compelling. Arthur was at the blackboard explaining some examples of how to solve algebraic equations, while Drew sat with one of the cooperative learning groups of students, equipped with paper and pencil. An inspiring teacher, schooled in advanced university math courses, Arthur was enthusiastic and very efficient at solving the given problems.

Drew, on the other hand, had a language arts background, and his techniques for teaching algebra needed some polishing. As Arthur demonstrated the solving of the questions, Drew frequently raised his hand and asked questions; "So, whatever you do to one side of the equation you have to do to the other?" "When you want to get rid of a number that is being subtracted do you add that number to both sides?" "What if there is a variable on both sides of the equation instead of just one?" As Drew asked questions the students began to make more and more inquiries about the problems. As Drew jotted down important points from the board, students took some notes in their binders. "If Mr. Dobie (Drew) is able to ask questions and make notes without being called stupid then I can too," is what I bet many of them were thinking. The interaction among students and teachers during that lesson was fantastic!

Later in the class, I made some even more interesting observations. The students who usually needed to be encouraged to take an active interest in math were seeking out Drew for help on the assigned questions. I believe they were able to relate to Drew as a fellow learner of math, which made him very approachable. The students who were already enthusiastic about math were, generally, drawn toward Arthur to discuss their work. Upon reflection, I realized how much sense this attraction to the two different teachers in the classroom made and I rushed over to talk to Arthur and Drew about it.

"How did you guys think of that technique in math class today?" I eagerly asked. "What technique?" Arthur asked. I explained what I had observed. "I was just trying to learn how to teach algebra again," Drew said.

---

How often do we feel the need to always have to "know"—to be the expert?

## Teacher as Expert

The "teacher as expert" role that is so endemic to schooling is often, paradoxically, an impediment to learning. Teachers are successful "products" of the systems of schooling. Conventional schooling salutes those who know with prizes, awards, rewards, high marks, and victory to the winners, and seemingly without care trivializes those who don't know through exclusion, spectator status, rejection, and feelings of being a loser. Young people are often left with the impression that adults know everything. Viewed another way, adults don't need to learn anymore once they've finished school. How often do we observe students, at the end of a school year, publicly discarding notebooks and binders, representing the records of a year's schoolwork? What does this tell us? "That's another year out of the way!" "I've learned that; I don't need it anymore." Clearly, Drew hadn't learned his mathematics and this was publicly demonstrated to the students. As Drew asked questions, pondered Arthur's replies and tried to make sense of his mathematical world, the students saw his inquiries as validation of their own lack of understanding.

Students who do not understand and who are, perhaps, average by our conventional classifications, are often reluctant to volunteer answers, let alone ask questions. They are afraid of appearing "dumb." Drew provided a antidote to this malaise of "dumbness". Here in the midst of a group of students was a teacher struggling to learn the same subject. Here was a teacher admitting he did not understand and openly displaying his lack of understanding. Drew was demonstrating much, much more than his lack of understanding of Arthur's mathematics. He was demonstrating that he was still a learner. He was demonstrating that teachers don't know everything. He was demonstrating that adults don't know everything.

## Teacher as Co-Learner

Freire (1988) speaks about the concept of "teacher as co-learner." This somewhat humbling view would challenge the more conventional practices of schooling, which are characterized by "teacher as expert," "teacher as controller of knowledge," power and control throughout the institution, and "teachers as controller of the curriculum." These practices breed dependency and compliance in students, but worse, they deny the liberation of young people in their learning. If we think about Drew's role in Arthur's math class there is an interesting confluence of thoughts. Drew's behavior caused the young people to see their "not knowing" in a more liberating light. The conventional institutional attitude of reluctance and reticence to inquire, to ask questions, for many of Arthur's students was breaking down when a teacher, a symbol of the institutional control, was in their midst doing just that. True liberation, of course, would have to move considerably further than the events in Arthur's class. If students were to truly experience learning for life, they would have to move toward owning their learning, connecting their learning to their lives, and posing problems in their relations with their world. It is this fundamental behavior of problem-posing education that requires that the teacher-student contradiction be resolved. "The teacher is no longer merely the-one-who-teaches, but one who is himself taught in dialogue with the students, who in turn while being taught also teach" (Freire, 1988, pp. 66–74).

Drew, in a superficial way, was beginning a process that could, with the right intention, lead to an enlightened change in the conventional teacher–student contradiction: the all-knowing–unknowing teacher–student relationships. The following journal excerpt from a fifth-grade teacher, Garry Jones, aptly demonstrates students' owning their learning, with teachers as co-learners.

> The all-school assembly Garry (his student teacher) and I organized partway through the school year was a moment filled with success, a moment when I could step out of the way and give it all to the students. . . .

The kids got into groups and worked on it Monday. The assembly is tomorrow (Thursday). It won't be a polished production . . . it will be kid made. Amazing things have happened.

Roxy and Charmaine simply took the jobs as co-hosts. They talked to other teachers who are involved, set the program, and wrote the introductions. Charmaine NEVER reads to the class and tomorrow she will read to 500 kids! Roxy just told her, I guess.

Vivian has organized a wonderful fashion show. The script has the right tone, mood, it sounds right. She trained all the girls (and two boys) and taught them how to walk. Vivian said that her mother is coming . . . for the first time ever!

Erica, Cynthia, and Amelia are doing a dance. They worked on this for many hours at home. Like, is this homework? Did I have to check it on a class list?

John is reading a poem which Jeffrey wrote, while four kids act it out.

All these leaders are NOT kids I would have chosen as leaders. They have shown abilities I did not suspect. . . .

Every child was involved in the assembly and it came off without a hitch. (Clandinin et al., 1993, p. 125)

The problem-posing approach to learning would require teachers to "move over," as Garry did in allowing his students to plan and orchestrate the whole-school assembly. Only in this way will young people experience learning that is connected to their lives and useful in helping them understand their world. A young man in tenth grade provides interesting comments on the teacher–student contradiction:

. . . but when you get to high school, you know, students are getting older and when you give them a choice and the responsibility and say, "OK, this is what you can do," they go for it, because they are given control of their education.

That doesn't only help in school. In the job, you're not always, you don't always have somebody standing over you and looking at you and telling you what to do. It helps everywhere, not just in school, in your life, at home, in your job, whatever you're doing. Not everything's going to be structured for you every single time you want to do something. So choice gives you an insight to take initiative and responsibility for your own learning and your own actions.

I think the students should take a little more responsibility for their learning and **the teachers should step back a little bit** [emphasis by the authors] because I think it may be easier for a student to learn from somebody who they can relate to better like at a better level, and you can say, "Yeah, hey, I can do that if he can do that." (Calgary Board of Education, 1991, unpublished transcript of Grade 12 Student Forum)

## Independence and Empowerment

Control continues to be an issue. The twelfth-grader is asking for freedom. He's asking for some control, for the opportunity to assume some responsibility, and for the chance to work alongside his teacher, rather than being constantly directed. The co-teaching concept, espoused by Freire, embraces the cooperative teacher–student relationship that young people seem to crave.

In their early years children are instinctive learners. Sensory experience satisfies basic human needs and moves quickly to embrace curiosity, inquisitiveness, and exploration, first through solitary activity, even among others, and then through increasing levels of social interaction. In the schooling context children have perhaps their greatest freedom in the kindergarten years, after which, paradoxically, the freedom tends to diminish. In their older years, young people are seeking independence and searching for opportunities to have some say in their lives. They react negatively to being constantly told what to do. What do schools tend to do in this regard? Our ways of learning have focused on "telling" and "making" students learn. These ways require the authority of the institution to be effective and many students tend to object. They dislike the relationships that become part of the "telling" and "making." A young woman from a high school provides a powerful statement on these kinds of relationships and the learning she prefers:

> . . . like if a student asks a question and the teacher explains it, and the student says, "Oh, I didn't really understand that, can you explain it to me again?" and they repeat exactly what they said, and it's just kind of like, you know, yo, I don't have a learning problem, I'm just not understanding what you're saying." And I think that teachers need to be more personal with the student, they need to work one-on-one a lot with students, get on a basis where they know how a student learns best, and that if a student's having trouble, it's not that they're dumb, you know, it's that the teacher, or the way the teacher explained it, didn't really apply to the way the student learns. I think that if the teachers took more time to work individually with students that were willing to meet one-on-one with them and learn the type of learning ability that they have, or whatever, so that they can explain to the student better, and I think that the student then develops more respect for the teacher, and they have a better relationship, and then the student will try harder for the teacher. (Calgary Board of Education, 1991, unpublished transcript of a Grade 12 Student Forum)

## Personalized Learning

The comments of this student remind us of the discussion in Chapter 3 regarding Bobby, Andrea, Debbie, and Joel seeking relationships with their teachers which benefited their learning. Nancy, in Chapter 2, seemed to reap similar benefits from her relationship with Tina. What is germane to our discussion is that through these relationships the young people experience more meaningful learning. They experienced learning with an infusion of humanness, and through this humanness the learning seemed more connected to their lives. Learning that is based on relationships reflects more personal behavior and more one-on-one time. It would be difficult to sustain "telling" and "making" in this kind of learning environment. Indeed the more personalized learning of which our young people speak implies their more intimate involvement. This in turn suggests a closer connection to life. As we keep in mind the co-learning and problem posing, the power and relevance of Freire's advice seems to receive strong affirmation. **Why do we seem to deny young people the opportunity to make connections between their learning and their lives?**

In Chapter 3 we invited readers to reflect on the ways teachers define young people. The stories of our two high school friends, Kathy, and the students who surrounded Drew, raise the interesting consideration of the ways young people define their teachers. We have understood for some time the importance of adult role models for young people. The teacher-as-learner concept is a rich extension of the more conventional notion of adult role model. The views expressed by our student contributors, captured nicely in the "move over a little" expression, sees the role model moving beyond the "knowledgeable, respectful, good-living, admirable person" view, to include a person who is still learning. **In what ways do you think you are defined by young people?** The question of defining people, especially within the schooling context, is never more exposed than when the assessment of learning and teaching is involved.

## Rehearsal and Application

Teachers teach with the intention that young people will learn, but how the effectiveness of learning is determined often leaves more questions than answers.

> Since the only learning that can be measured without ambiguity is recall, we have, implicitly, if not explicitly, reached the conclusion that the measure of recall is a measure of learning. As a consequence, virtually the entire teaching–learning process is centered around the presentation, memorization, and recall of facts. (Clarke in Costa et al., 1992)

This incisive comment points at a troublesome aspect of our schooling systems. If a child is playing hockey we tend to judge performance by watching the child play hockey. Similarly, if a child is learning dance our evaluations reside in observing the child performing dance. So it is with most of life's endeavors. In life-related pursuits, learning may be viewed as an interplay between rehearsal and free-form experience. Opportunities are provided to "rehearse" skills and abilities that are part of the ultimate purpose for the learning. Throughout the rehearsals there are constant chances for application to the ultimate purpose in free-form, unfettered ways. The hockey player plays hockey, the young dancer performs, a gymnast competes, a driver education student drives on the streets, and a young person learning the follies of warfare must understand the lessons for life and society in useful ways. Whatever the pursuit, the coach, instructor, parent, or teacher guides, helps, nurtures, and generally facilitates the young person doing things themselves, to the point that they become increasingly confident, capable, and competent.

In school our conventions determine success in learning using measures that are mostly unrelated to actual demonstrations of learning; they do not allow a young person the opportunity to demonstrate what has been learned in a real sense. Students are almost indoctrinated in the psychometric modes of learning measurement—short-answer quizzes, multiple-choice tests, fill-in-the-blanks, power tests, percentage–letter grades, computer-scored test sheets, and so on.

---

⤳ WE HAD BEEN TALKING, AS A STAFF, about broad-based assessment for some time. Reliance on pencil-and-paper, short-answer tests simply did not provide young people with opportunities to demonstrate what they had learned. They had no choices in what they learned and 65% on a multiple choice test had rather limited meaning. We thought long and hard about how to approach the matter. How do we give young people some choice? How do we encourage application of concepts and understandings from their academic subjects? How do we "invite" teachers to participate? After much discussion, planning, and reflection we established a trial period of six weeks, during which students would have Wednesday afternoons to plan and implement their learning choices. Teacher advisers were appointed and the necessary administrative procedures established. On these afternoons students would be free to work in school, or anywhere in the city, to meet learning goals that they had agreed on with their advisers. They had all been involved in establishing their evaluation plans and each student would have the right to award 50% of the final mark.

Students were assembled in the cafeteria for the announcement. The reaction was mixed. "How many pages do we have to write?" "What will 'it' be worth on the final exam?" "Where are we going to find the time to do all this 'extra' work?" "You mean I can really decide the topic I want to learn about?" The questions were endless. Our attitude was supportive, helpful, patient, and patient again!

The first weeks were a struggle, but slowly and very interestingly the attitude changed. Students gradually became enthusiastic. Time was used in a variety of ways. Many were learning in various parts of the city and the ways of presenting their learning differed widely. Students used every nook and cranny of the school in which to learn. We had communicated well with parents before the experiment commenced, but even in the throes of reality not one negative reaction was received.

During the actual exhibition period each student or group (no more than three to a group) had to book time in front of an evaluation committee made up of teachers and parents (no more than three to an evaluation committee). This was perhaps one of the most exciting parts of the activity. Students presented demonstrations of learning that were extremely impressive. Passionate demonstrations on topics ranging from sexual promiscuity to the ethics of gambling on remote-controlled car racing provided outstanding statements from impressive young people.

One of the most interesting outcomes was the extremely positive feedback into the community from the parents who were involved in the evaluations. This showed the importance of parents being a part of change, rather than simply being told about it.

---

The reactions of students in the story are typical. "How many pages do we have to write?" "What will 'it' be worth on the final exam?" "Where are we going to find the time to do all this 'extra' work?" Their history of putting in a block of weeks in class preparatory to a test, to determine how successfully they had learned their work, was part of their pattern of schooling. Sit down, write the test, hope for the best . . . what next!

## Negotiation and Voice

Students seldom have voice in decisions about their learning. Students have little or no opportunity to negotiate. The young people in our story were being given that opportunity. Certainly they had not done this before, but then, neither had the teachers. The action was based on the belief and conviction that young people need a say in what they learn and how they learn it, and a real opportunity to demonstrate their learning. The experience was in the nature of experiment, but it was controlled and somewhat cautious. In any of these situations there is an element of "ready, fire, aim," but not in a cavalier fashion. Much preparatory work had been done by way of reading and discussion. Parents had been informed and their input invited. Students had been involved. They had even collectively designed their evaluation process. But there is nothing like the reality of the real thing! Student disbelief is coupled with the conventional performance requirements and the powerful draw toward regularized practice presents a massive hurdle to overcome. In spite of best laid plans, reality brings its hesitancy.

> So what did happen when we asked our students to design the perfect class? They began by suggesting ideas independently. Next, they shared their thoughts, in small groups, writing them on large sheets of butcher paper we had hung around the room. Finally, four elected representatives led a discussion of the ideas and organized them into a draft of a class constitution, including guidelines for group work, late work and day-to-day life in the classroom.

> The biggest obstacle was the students' disbelief that we were really going to live by the policy. Five days into the year a student stopped by my desk and asked, "Are you guys really going to use these policies, or did we do this just as an exercise to see what it's like to make up rules?" (Smith, 1993, p. 36)

In spite of the real opportunity to negotiate and plan, students were still somewhat skeptical. In both stories attempts to empower students met with a certain amount of disbelief. This is a compelling reason that change must be founded on beliefs and assumptions that have been honed with the benefit of information, reflection, and construction.

Teachers and students in the stories both experienced opportunities to assume ownership and responsibility and to implement through negotiation. They were able to make sense out of things through having voice, choice, and construction of knowledge and meaning. Teachers supported, facilitated, and guided, but above all they "moved over a little" allowing students to "do."

It is fundamental to effective learning that learners can and must make decisions about what they learn, and they must process and interpret content individually to make it meaningful. This view of learners and of learning, reflected to varying degrees in our stories, is premised in the social construction of knowledge and meaning.

> The first question that most teachers ask when they begin to write a lesson plan is: What do I want the students to learn? The way a teacher answers this question reflects his or her assumptions about the nature of learning, and obviously will have a significant impact on both what is taught and how it is taught.
>
> A generation of teachers has been trained to answer this question in terms of behavioral and instructional objectives. Such objectives represent, by definition, terminal behaviors on the part of the learner that are demonstrable and quantifiable. (Clarke, in Costa et al., 1992, p. 28)

Learning that is connected to life, learning that is meaningful for young people, must involve the youngsters in authentic ways. It is not acceptable for the teacher to ask solely, "What do I want the students to learn?" This somewhat authoritarian, teacher-as-expert stance denies the humanness of students. It is a position based on the assumption that the older, wiser, more competent teacher as adult-in-authority, purports to know what is best for young people. Young people come to school to learn and their learning must help them understand themselves and their world, so that their lives are richer. In a general sense, learning helps young people to understand the connectedness of things; to understand life. The fragmentation that is evident in school learning does not contribute to this purpose. The "making" and "telling" that is almost endemic to our learning environments, is based on the rather arrogant assumption that the adults-in-authority know best what our young people will become. No, as we approach this most moral of obligations it is our profound responsibility to invite, inspire, and accompany young people in their becoming— unique individuals who will enrich not only their own world, but ours as well.

## AN INVITATION TO THE READER

The following page suggests a process for thinking about the chapter, to stimulate conversation, encourage debate, share stories, provoke further questions, challenge current thinking, or engage in further personal reflection. University classes, professional development groups, school staffs, and parent groups may find the chapter's questions and related text useful, as a challenge to personal beliefs, understandings and experiences, toward affirmation or change.

We present the concept of "filter." Readers are invited to consider the central question of the chapter, along with the questions that arise from the text. It is not our intention to limit or reduce context to one small portion of the chapter—we are conscious of the problem of reductionism. It is our hope that, as readers proceed through the book, they will respond to questions in a more holistic manner.

The concept of filter is a metaphor for the reader's personal beliefs, values, and experiences, through which new ideas are explored and current beliefs challenged. It is this filtering that provides an opportunity for the reader to make personal connections to the questions and ideas in the chapter. This process may provide an opportunity to deepen meaning and understanding of the concepts and ideas discussed.

**In the following framework, you are invited to contemplate your beliefs, understandings, and experiences through reflecting on the questions and related text in Chapter 4.**

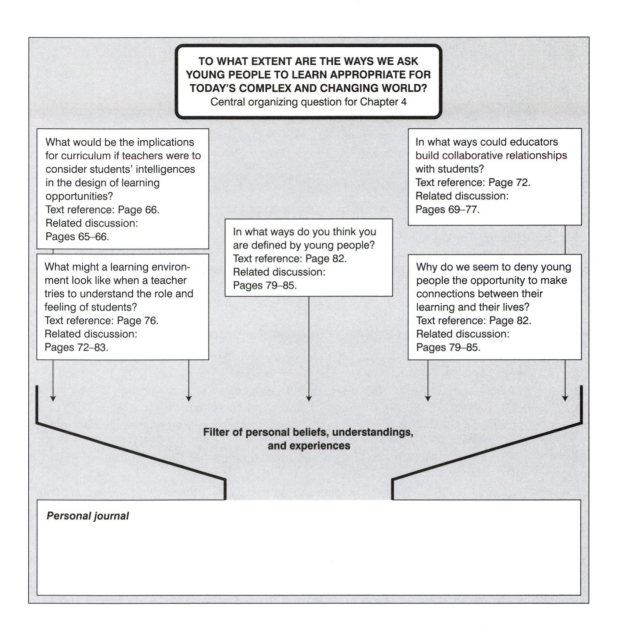

**TO WHAT EXTENT ARE THE WAYS WE ASK YOUNG PEOPLE TO LEARN APPROPRIATE FOR TODAY'S COMPLEX AND CHANGING WORLD?**
Central organizing question for Chapter 4

What would be the implications for curriculum if teachers were to consider students' intelligences in the design of learning opportunities?
Text reference: Page 66.
Related discussion: Pages 65–66.

In what ways could educators build collaborative relationships with students?
Text reference: Page 72.
Related discussion: Pages 69–77.

What might a learning environment look like when a teacher tries to understand the role and feeling of students?
Text reference: Page 76.
Related discussion: Pages 72–83.

In what ways do you think you are defined by young people?
Text reference: Page 82.
Related discussion: Pages 79–85.

Why do we seem to deny young people the opportunity to make connections between their learning and their lives?
Text reference: Page 82.
Related discussion: Pages 79–85.

**Filter of personal beliefs, understandings, and experiences**

*Personal journal*

# REFERENCES

Black, S. (1994, January). Different kinds of smart. *The Executive Educator, 26.*

Brooks, J., & Brooks, M. (1993*). In search of understanding: The case for constructivist classrooms.* Alexandria, VA.: Association for Supervision and Curriculum Development.

Clandinin, J. (1993). *Learning to teach, teaching to learn.* New York: Teachers College Press.

Costa, A. et al. (Eds.). (1992). If minds matter: A foreword to the future. Palatine, IL: Skylight Publishing, Inc.

Duckworth, E. (1987). *The having of wonderful ideas and other essays on teaching and learning.* New York: Teachers College Press.

Freire, P. (1988*). Pedagogy of the oppressed.* New York: Continuum.

Gardner, H. (1993). *Multiple intelligences: The theory and practice.* New York: Basic Books.

Greene, M. (1986). Landscapes and meanings. *Language Arts, 63*(8), 776–783.

Kohn, A. (1993). Choices for children: Why and how to let students decide. *Phi Delta Kappan, 75*(1), 8–20.

Leinhardt, G. (1992). What research on learning tells us about teaching. *Educational Leadership, 49*(7).

Paley, V. (1991). The heart and soul of the matter: Teaching as a moral act. *Educational Forum, 55*(2), 155–166.

Senge, P. (1990, Fall). The leader's new work: Building learning organizations. *Sloan Management Review,* 7–23.

Smith, K. (1993, October). Becoming the guide on side. *Educational Leadership, 51*(2), 35–37.

Smith, L., & Johnson, H. (1993). Control in the classroom: Listening to adolescent voices. *Language Arts, 70*(1), 18–30.

Taylor, F. (1911). *The principles of scientific management.* New York: W. W. Norton & Company.

# SUGGESTED READINGS

FREDERICK J. ABEL and JEAN P. ABEL (1996), in a paper titled "Integrating Mathematics and Social Studies: Activities Based on Internet Resources," challenge the notion, often helped by students, that academic disciplines are distinct and separate. Their paper, presented to the Annual Meeting of the Montana Council of Teachers of Mathematics, gives examples of the ways in which teachers can integrate the disciplines of mathematics and social studies. They focus on meaningful integration that allows students to construct their own knowledge based on their interaction with peers, teachers, and the Internet.

Connecting learning to life and exploring integrative understandings of curriculum often require a paradigm shift in teaching and learning. "Shifting Paradigms: Emerging Issues for Educational Policy and Practice," an article by JOHN FISCHETTI and others (1996), creates a framework for understanding the paradigm shift. The new paradigm shift is based on cognitive development research and constructivist theory.

Three articles in the 1995 journal *Theory into Practice, 34*(2) provide interesting discussion on student voice in learning. FLORENCIA GARCIA and others (pp. 138–144) present a dialogue among three student co-researchers who participated in a research project about their motivation to learn. The students discuss, among other things, what it meant to them to have voice. MICHAEL O'LOUGHLIN examines circumstances under which teachers might define themselves as keyholders of culture, who unmask authoritative knowledge and cultural domination (pp. 107–116). In this context, his article discusses the importance of student voice, along with critical teaching and democracy in education. The third article, "Voices We Want to Hear and Voices We Don't," by PETER H. JOHNSTON and JOHN G. NICHOLS (pp. 94–100) posits that students need empowerment to have a voice in curriculum design and governance. Their position that the fostering of student voice requires schools to establish conditions for democratic talk in classes, is particularly consistent with our discussion.

Readers may be interested in the 2nd edition (1996) of ELEANOR DUCKWORTH'S book, *The Having of Wonderful Ideas and other Essays on Teaching and Learning,* published through Teachers College Press.

# 5

# A LIVED CURRICULUM

## An Invitation . . .

We now invite the reader to consider who makes decisions about curriculum and who is consulted. Often, curriculum materials such as kits, packages, and teaching guides are planned by someone outside the classroom and merely transmitted by the teacher to the student. The consequences of such an approach are a focus on the management of time, people, and resources, as opposed to relevancy and connectedness. We suggest that this process, dominated by power and control, tends to deny the individuality, uniqueness, and voice of students and teachers.

**How might we understand curriculum in a way that respects the wisdom and experience of both teachers and students?**

The chapter considers curriculum as holistic, emanating from an understanding of and respect for the humanness of young people. Curriculum should be defined by the experience, knowledge, and understanding that young people bring to the classroom. This voice in the curriculum makes connections between lived experiences and the rigorous requirements of the curriculum guides. The chapter concludes with the position that young people need authentic opportunities to rehearse and demonstrate learning that is connected to their lives.

≈ I WAS IN THE STAFF ROOM AT LUNCHTIME, a few months into my first year of teaching, when Mary Schultz, a veteran language arts teacher, sat down with me. Mary offered me access to any of her eighth-grade language arts units and invited me down to her classroom after lunch. I was pleased by her helpfulness and soon made my way to her room. Her shelves were lined with labeled binders according to grade level and unit title. She led me to the eighth-grade section, described many of the units, and finally recommended that if I hadn't done a novel study yet, I should use her *Ten Little Indians* binder. The binder was full of chapter questions, quizzes, and book report projects. I thanked her and with the huge binder in tow made my way to my own room.

A few weeks later I had a similar experience with Verna Robinson, a math teacher on staff. Verna invited me to come and have a look at her math work for seventh and ninth grade, the classes I was teaching. Once again I entered a classroom filled with precisely labeled binders and left with a few that were recommended.

As a person new to the school and to teaching I welcomed the connection to other teachers. But I wondered whether these units would work as well for me or my class. I had so many questions about how to plan so that it was interesting and meaningful for all of the students. The binders were a help but they didn't answer my "big picture" questions about curriculum.

What is the "big picture" of curriculum alluded to in the story? The word *curriculum* is derived from a Latin word meaning "course" or "path." For us this implies curriculum as a journey for students in school. In Chapter 4, we discussed young people in the process of becoming, a concept that recognizes their individuality and humanity. If a teacher were to create a place where this process of becoming could flourish, curriculum would have to be more than kits, packages, and generic binders of materials, with a considerably different design. Curriculum, as a journey for each student, seems to fit with this process of becoming. Individuality and the uniqueness of young people and teachers seem to be denied when curriculum is delivered through kits and packages.

## CURRICULUM AND CONTROL

In previous chapters we have recognized the influence of Taylor (1911) on the institution of schooling. His ideas of applying advanced production methods have had a lasting effect on curriculum. Students are faced with one teaching package after another in one subject after another, in a manner similar to a factory assembly line. As teaching units are passed from teacher to teacher, stagnation of curriculum sets in. Our story illustrates this conventional understanding of and approach to curriculum implementation. **How did we arrive at a curriculum dependent on preplanned teaching packages, which deny the voices and experience of young people and teachers?**

## Fragmentation and Unconnectedness

Schools have become managed in such a way that production methods are honored, resulting in curriculum that has become specialized, fragmented, and narrow in focus. Moffet (1994) speaks to this issue of fragmentation with his view that "a strong case can be made that the pre-organization of curriculum into courses accounts for the ineffectuality of schooling" (p. 204). In the story, the teacher is given two entirely different and unconnected binders—one for language arts and one for math. The binders not only lacked connection, but their contents also were not connected to the experience of the teacher and her students.

1. Are there not some ties, some interweaving of literal and numerical systems?
2. Could one be used to gain a deeper understanding of the other?

3. And perhaps most important, could the voices, interests, and questions of the students help make these connections between courses and subject areas?

Rather than be guided by such questions, schools—especially secondary schools—continue to cycle students through subject area courses that have few connections to one another or to the lives of young people. Does this system for managing and organizing people and curriculum result in the most effective learning for young people?

How can we work with one another, with teachers like the one in the story, to understand and practice a more dynamic curriculum? Could teachers work more collaboratively to improve the totality of learning experiences young people have at school? Perhaps understandings of curriculum may then be based on beliefs about learning and the nature of young people in ways that respect the wisdom and experience of both teachers and students. The fragmentation and unconnectedness of curriculum might be reduced if teachers and students were both engaged in its design.

---

∾   THE HIGH SCHOOL INFORMATION BOOKLET was impressive. Beliefs, purpose, vision, expectations, program descriptions, schedules, and general school philosophy. Anybody with interest in the school was given a copy. I had been given mine many months before I engaged in conversations with the school about curriculum and its development in the building.

The principal and I had a number of discussions about curriculum, and she had explained to me how the school was addressing the problem of fragmentation. Opportunities were provided for students to engage in cross-curricular learning one day a week but it was not working very well. All too often teachers were giving students subject area work to 'catch up' and seldom were students taught the skills necessary to draw connections between their subject learnings. I drew the principal's attention to some of the beliefs and concepts in the school information booklet and asked if any attention had been given to the implied meanings and understandings.

"To some extent, but not in any great detail," was the guarded reply.

"I wonder," I said, "whether teachers are understanding these published concepts and beliefs to the point where they are incorporating them into their practice?" This was a rhetorical question, of course, for clearly the teachers were not. What to do?

At another meeting the subject of curriculum was discussed. If teachers are to encourage students to make connections between subjects, to apply their learnings to life-related questions and issues, shouldn't attention be given to a whole-school curriculum model that would describe the school's approach to learning?

Shouldn't the teachers be engaging in reflective practice to professionally challenge their beliefs and assumptions about learning and teaching? What about the published beliefs and philosophy in the school's information booklet? What about "multiplicity of learning needs," "student-centered," "lifelong learning," "contribute to a global society," "student and teacher empowerment," "multicultural," "learning as the construction of meaning," and "self-directed learning," to name only a few? We agreed that a model typical of the kind required would be designed and brought to a future meeting for discussion only.

The model was duly designed and brought to the school for the next meeting. "Interesting," said the principal. "I can see what you mean. We can't expect the students to work in cross-disciplinary ways when perhaps the staff are unskilled in these ways of learning. I can see what needs to be done, but where do we find the time?"

Curriculum should have its architecture. Without this it is but a collection of pieces. What is fundamental is the need for whole-school curriculum architecture to have the appropriate pedagogy. The principal and I concluded our last meeting with the agreement that he would give the matter some more thought.

There is a trite little adage which suggests that "life doesn't present itself in subject areas." This story describes a school where the curriculum is an array of subjects, from which students choose according to a timetable. Teachers are given teaching assignments made up of subjects in which they specialize. Any connections between subjects is left to those who are perhaps least able to make them—the students! The school's information literature provides strong statements about purpose, goals, objectives, and beliefs. Concepts such as "student centered," "multicultural," "contribute to a global society," "multiplicity of learning needs," "student and teacher empowerment," "learning is the construction of meaning," "self-directed learners," and "lifelong learning" provide only a partial list. But nowhere do these concepts appear to be receiving attention. The school curriculum is lived each day, but the young people do not experience a "lived" curriculum. What the school declares in its literature is not, in fact, what the school delivers in its daily fare of course offerings. This may sound like harsh judgment. Clearly, as in most schools, competent, conscientious teachers engage students in learning with considerable success. But the question remains: **To what extent should a curriculum be seamless and connected, such that young people come to more clearly understand their world?** To what extent is the curriculum a "lived curriculum" in ways that invite young people to lend the curriculum [their] lives? (Greene, 1971)

## CURRICULUM FRAMEWORK

Terms such as *seamless* and *connected* evoke understandings of holistic think-ing and questions of intention arise. **What benefits are intended for young people through the way a curriculum is conceived, organized, and experienced?** How will they progress toward becoming more competent peo-ple, more contented members of their peer group and more contributing mem-bers of society? Would the young people attending the school in our story achieve these benefits? To what extent is curriculum fragmented, uninviting, and adult-serving? Seldom is curriculum thought out and planned as a whole school. Usually, time is the primary organizer. In high schools the Carnegie unit prescribes 25 hour units of learning time on which course credit is based. At other grade levels, minimum learning time in subjects is often set by gov-ernment and school jurisdictions. Schools then take these requirements and organize school days to fit. What about the overall plan for a school? Do we ever sit down and ask questions such as:

1. What is the world of young people like?
2. How can we invite young people to learn through experiences that enrich their lives?
3. How can we design learning experiences, which make connections among subject learning, so that opportunities exist for young people to apply learning to their lives?
4. How can we involve young people in the design and planning of their curriculum?

A curriculum is simply a framework within which learning occurs. It is not a rigid, prescriptive framework but rather a holistic guideline shaped by agree-ments, beliefs, requirements and needs. A framework should provide a basic understanding of a curriculum's intent.

## Holistic Curriculum

A holistic curriculum would begin with a statement about the whole to provide a context within which the parts, as they are learned, could be understood in relationship to each other and to the whole (Clarke, in Costa, et al., 1993). "In order to understand anything we must have a sense of the fundamental con-nections which form the backdrop of all existence" (Salk, in Costa et al., 1993, p. 36). Clarke speaks further on the matter of the whole being greater than the sum of its parts, with the position that "without an understanding of the whole as a context to endow them with meaning, the parts are essentially worthless" (p. 36). The school in the previous story could learn from these comments. The "fundamental connections" within the school's curriculum needed attention. The goal of "opportunities for cross-curricular learning one day a week" was not working well because not only were the fundamental connections absent, but so were attention to the fundamental concepts that needed to permeate teacher practice. In short, the school lacked clarity in a holistic view of their curriculum. Their understanding of curriculum lacked any sense of architecture.

---

RITA McPELK WAS A TEACHER most of us would have been proud to have as a friend. She was about 60 years old, kind, thoughtful, and friendly. The children in her third-grade class were almost like her grandchildren.

Charly, Ben, Jason, and Gwen were in her class, but they were other people's grandchildren. Hellions, the four of them. Rita's kindness and thoughtfulness didn't work with them—and they wouldn't be good in class! The infamous four stood out like sore thumbs. Often they would be either standing in the hallway, behind Rita's in-class discipline screen, or outside the principal's office. Rita had other students with whom she had difficulties, but her firm and friendly grandmotherly touch would usually defuse the problems.

Most of Rita's difficulties with her children arose from her rigidity. Her kids liked art, but when the allotted 45 minutes was up, there was clean-up time and then on to something completely different. Math was next. Blackboard explanations of double digit numbers to add and subtract, followed by worksheets for drill and practice. Interest was difficult to sustain in this subject so Rita had to be very strict; children had to be "made" to learn. Some of her third-grade children were frightened.

Language arts followed math, and out came phonics books and basal readers. The hellions were now making their presence felt. Rita was distracted, the other children were distracted, and the principal again was called on to solve the problem.

Not only was Rita struggling to engage her students, she was paying no attention to any connections between the subjects her children were being made to learn, nor to any connections between the learning and her children's lives. The whole had no context. And if her principal did not deal with her miscreants effectively, he would be at fault. After all, she was kind, friendly, firm, and organized. She was not responsible for the children's upbringing.

---

The "making" and "telling" of which Moffett (1994) speaks seemed to be at work in Rita McPelk's classroom. She taught from the perspective of her world into which her children were required to fit. Rita was a good person. She was a conscientious teacher who genuinely wanted the best for her children. The problem for Rita was that it was she and she alone who decided what the "best" was. There was no larger context for her program plans or her requirements for her children. Conceptions of holistic curriculum were foreign and as a result there was no larger context within which meaning could be bestowed on the parts. Her children were made to learn unconnected parts, and their lack of engagement created constant problems in her class. The questions posed on page 96 would have been useful for Rita to reflect on her practice. She needed a fundamental curriculum framework within which to work; a framework to provide architecture for her teaching and the children's learning.

*Framework, fundamental connections,* and *curriculum architecture* are terms that describe the primary activity in designing a lived curriculum. It is primary in that other decisions, plans, and actions flow from the understandings embedded within. The high school in our story appeared to have a framework, through its information booklet, but it did not translate into day-to-day reality. "Anybody with interest in the school was given a copy," but, "seldom were students taught the skills necessary to draw connections between their subject learnings."

If these fundamental considerations for a lived curriculum are to be present and active, (1) they must be determined, designed, and understood by students, teachers, and parents,(2) they must constitute the primary reference for the design and practice of the parts, and (3) they must receive constant attention, through reflective practice, for their inherent meaning, knowledge, beliefs, values, and implications for learning.

Rita McPelk's school lacked these fundamental considerations for a lived curriculum. Her plans for learning suffered, therefore, along with the collective sense of direction and orchestration for learning and teaching in her school. Of particular note is the need for understanding by students. One of the difficulties experienced by the high school in the story was the lack of understanding by teachers of the school's philosophical intentions. Of equal importance was the absence of student involvement. If students have never experienced these ways of learning, then nothing magical will happen to suddenly spark their enthusiasm. Meaning and understanding will occur slowly, but with genuine connection to life we can be sure that it will occur.

## Deepening Understandings of Curriculum

Holistic curriculum frameworks "make sense only when the full reality of learning and teaching is taken into account" (British National Commission on Education, 1993, p. 47). Frameworks, of themselves, are essentially prosaic statements with prescriptive overtones. They make sense only when they are "owned" by a particular learning community and when members of that community have meaning and understanding of their deeper structures. The British Commission of Education presents an interesting framework:

**Our School Curriculum:**

- will motivate [students] towards learning and promote enjoyment in learning. It will do this by such means as challenging [students] and arousing their curiosity, by helping them both to acquire and to use the basic tools of communication, by opening out aesthetic and other experiences to which they can respond, by providing learning which individuals perceive as relevant to their own present or future needs and by helping them to mature as confident and self-reliant members of society;

- will challenge the acceptance of low expectations and low aspirations too often found in our system. Thus it will offer schools and teachers support and encouragement, and will in particular give them scope for creativity and innovation. It is the task of teachers to provide schemes of work best suited to the range of abilities and needs represented in any group of [students];

- will aim to be appealing to all [students], and will therefore be varied enough to enable each to develop his or her own range of 'intelligences' or abilities;

- will provide for progression, and will therefore follow naturally on from [preschool] education and will lead naturally on to further of higher education or employment and training;

- will provide a basis for measuring the attainment of young people;

- above all, will offer to all [students] a means of succeeding and having that success recognized. (pp. 47–48)

Consider some of the key phrases and their implications for a "lived" curriculum: "promote enjoyment in learning," "learning which individuals perceive as relevant to their own present and future needs," "will aim to be appealing to all [students] . . . to develop his or her own range of 'intelligences' or abilities," "offer to all [students] a means of succeeding and having that success recognized." These are powerful statements. However the power is not in the words, but in the meaning, understanding, and application.

In Chapter 2 the importance of beliefs, assumptions, and mental models as potentials pitfalls was presented in our ongoing quest for effective learning. As our "mental models, or mindscapes, are uncovered and challenged we may find that what for each of us is at the heart of education—our beliefs—are not lived out in our daily lives in school" (Chapter 2, p. 31). This "problem" is at the heart of change. It rears its head in the translation of statements into practice, and in the story it was problematic for the teachers. There are two dimensions to the problem: (1) the tacitness of many of our assumptions about learning and teaching, and (2) the reluctance of schools to dedicate time for teachers to engage in reflective practice, let alone reflection in practice. The school in the story engaged in many hours of time together to develop and craft the statements for their information brochure. But it was an intellectual exercise only. Once the work was done and the brochure published, the teachers got on with the business of doing what they had been doing for years—and in the same old ways. We are not suggesting that "the same old ways" are necessarily bad. We are suggesting that new concepts—concepts that were not in our knowledge base, say, five years ago—demand rigorous attention to meaning and understanding. We often hear voices in schools that discredit new concepts with dismissive remarks, such as, "It sounds just like the stuff we used to do in the '60s," "We've done that before," or "It's just another fad." Comments like these constitute a massive disservice to young people.

For a curriculum to be truly lived, we must " . . . invite, inspire, and accompany young people in their becoming. . . . " (Chapter 4, p. 85) as they pursue their learning journey. A lived curriculum must be connected to life, and such connections cannot be mandated. If an authority commanded you to like something, would you? Perhaps you would not admit to dislike if the authority exercised control. You would probably swallow the command like some bitter pill. Why would we expect youngsters to be any different? If, as the British Commission states, the curriculum would aim to be appealing to all students, enabling them to develop their own range of intelligences or abilities, then a lived curriculum must invite and inspire young people to lend that curriculum their lives.

&#x223d; MY TEAM-TEACHING PARTNER AND I left our curriculum meeting distraught about the prospect of teaching another unit revolving around a textbook. We sat in our classroom discussing our realization that if we were students we would hate to do the assignments and would be generally turned off by the upcoming Brazil unit.

"I understand where the rest of the team is coming from," I said. "There are some important concepts and factual pieces of information that need to be covered. However, there must be a way to design this unit that will interest students and at the same time educate them."

"I agree", Ms. Rumple said. "I don't understand why the rest of our team didn't like my suggestion of a KWL approach. I'm really tired of people viewing curriculum as something we need to get through, or simply cover.

"Maybe they didn't quite understand it," I said. "Could you tell me more about it?"

"I think it's important to see what the students KNOW about Brazil to start with—that's the 'K' part," Ms. Rumple said. "Some students may have some valuable background knowledge about Brazil that may contribute to the unit. The 'W' simply asks the students WHAT they are interested in exploring and learning about in this unit. The 'L' is part of the assessment phase, where the students demonstrate what is being LEARNED."

"That sounds like an interesting approach," I said. "But what if the students want to explore things that don't match the prescribed programs of study?"

"After seeing what kind of background the students have in Brazil—the 'K' phase—the teacher exposes students to as many facets of Brazil as possible," she said. "Their interest is piqued about the unit and at the same time key curriculum concepts are taught. Students may then pursue a concept in greater detail during the 'W' phase."

"So the students do not simply say, 'Hey, this what I'm doing today in regards to Brazil'?"

"No, far from it." Ms. Rumple said. "This approach requires a curriculum framework, or design, that explicitly outlines skills and concepts that are desired as unit outcomes. The key is determining the role of the students and incorporating their voice into the curriculum plan."

"Let's give your idea a chance," I said. "For the sake of the students it is worth exploring a new way of approaching this unit."

We wonder how many teachers like Ms. Rumple are frustrated with the view of curriculum as "ground to be covered," or something to be delivered, as opposed to a broader concept of curriculum that begins with a focus on the learner. The view of curriculum as something to be covered neglects the extent to which learning experiences are affected by students' needs, interests, and choices. Ms. Rumple, as she promotes the KWL approach to the Brazil unit, recognizes these experiences as valuable.

In Chapter 1 we indicated that societal changes are occurring at an alarming rate, while schools seem to be having grave difficulty adapting. The Information Age is here, but how has the nature of our curriculum responded? Ms. Rumple seems to be encountering a team of teachers who interpret curriculum to mean a finely specified, sequentially prescribed body of topics and learning outcomes, which all students must address the same way. The Information Age tells us that no one student can learn all the facts there are to know about a given topic. So should we not look at asking our young people to learn fewer things in greater depth and with greater connectedness?

## Negotiated Curriculum

Ms. Rumple and her colleague believe there must be a negotiated balance between what the teacher thinks the student needs to know (the "K" phase) and what the student would like to explore (the "W" phase). It seems to follow that curriculum can be shaped by both the teachers' expertise and judgment and the students' experience and voice. In this way the question, not the fact, becomes the foundation of the curriculum. **How would young people benefit from teachers who design curriculum according to their students' needs and interests?**

If we delve deeper into Ms. Rumple's KWL approach to the Brazil unit we begin to see the emergence of three aspects of curriculum. The "K," or knowledge, phase is connected to what the literature refers to as the intended, or planned, curriculum in concert with the background knowledge that students already possess. This is where the objectives, knowledge, skills, and attitudes that curriculum planners have developed are embedded. The "W" phase connects with what Aoki (1991) calls the curriculum as lived experience. This experienced curriculum exists within the context of the classroom and other learning environments. Students lend the curriculum their life within the experienced curriculum. It emerges from the planned curriculum and spontaneous personal connections the students make to their lives.

The experienced, lived curriculum is also a function of students' active participation in decisions regarding their learning. As a result of individual interests, needs, and abilities, the lived curriculum is different for each student in the classroom. Undoubtedly, during the "W" phase, the role of the student is important, but what about the role of the teacher? In Chapter 4 we referenced Freire's concept of teacher as "co-learner." For this to be apparent the notion of who is learning in schools must be expanded beyond the student. Teachers would no longer be all-knowing gatekeepers of knowledge who simply disseminate information. Nor would they be sparkling instructional wizards. Instead, they would be fully professional guides, facilitating learning by helping young people question and explore their world.

The "L," or learned, phase could be associated with what is called the attained curriculum. This is where the knowledge, skills, and attitudes that students acquire, as a result of the planned and lived curriculum, are assessed. While assessment of student outcomes is often guided by the planned curriculum, we need to recognize that valuable learning may occur as a result of the connection students are able to make to their own lives. This unplanned learning may be as important to the development of our young people as the learning intended by the curriculum as plan. It is important for teachers to be aware of and search for balance among these three aspects of curriculum when they design a unit.

In our story Ms. Rumple discusses the importance of determining the role of the students and incorporating their voice into the curriculum. "The benefits of self-determination and choice for students are compelling" (Chapter 4, p. 70). Students are concerned about the lack of control over their lives, and want some freedom to choose what they learn and with whom they learn it. Allowing students a voice in curriculum provides an immediate and valued manifestation of the concept "freedom of choice." It further encourages learning that values student individuality and diversity. **To what extent should curriculum include the voices and prior experiences of students?**

Young people are naturally curious about who they are and how they fit into their ever-changing and expanding world. They are seeking independence and searching for opportunities to have some say in their lives. We wonder if young people often think that the world outside school is unconnected to the world of the classroom, where in many instances textbook and worksheet learning prevail. As educators we must ask ourselves: **How can we develop a curriculum framework that sees a balance between young people actively exploring and questioning their world and the need to meet the program requirements of local jurisdictions?**

THE NINTH-GRADE ASSIGNMENTS involved choice for students in learning social studies. There were, however, some conditions. We gathered round, as a class, and talked about quality. What is good work? What is acceptable as good work? Our discussion ranged from standards for note and record books; plans for use of time; organization for research; collecting, synthesizing, and applying research; and finally, quality in presentation. Interestingly, as the discussion developed, students began to take over. "Come on, Jim, you know that's not a good idea, if you were a teacher would you accept that?" "If you can't read it after you've written it, why would you hand it in?"

A particularly progressive voice suggested, "We should somehow get together and decide ourselves whether our stuff is good enough to hand in to Mrs. Plimpton." And so the discussion continued with the students engrossed in determining their own standards for quality. I must admit to surprise, not that students were discussing this topic but that they were discussing it with such intensity. After a somewhat guarded and guided beginning, I was able to simply sit, observe, and listen.

When things were coming to a close and a short period of silence reigned, a lone voice was heard to say, "Mrs. Plimpton, you've heard what we've been saying and you've seen what we've written on the board; if somebody hands something in that's not good enough, don't accept it." Don't accept it. And this came from students.

We wrote up the points the students listed on the blackboard and I added a number of my own requirements. The information was published for the class and posted in the room.

The work began. Our plans called for periodic checks of individual work and periodic consultations with groups of students. It was at these points that the "rubber hit the road" as the saying goes. When Johnny Brosz waltzed up with work for my review, he was told quite clearly that it was not acceptable. But the power in my message was as much in the student-determined standards as in my own message. Later that afternoon a phone call came from Johnny's mother. Johnny had convinced her that he had been unjustly treated. After a somewhat frustrating call I invited her to visit me at school to discuss the matter more personally.

She came the next day and I took her to the classroom. I could have taken a stand from the position of my professional role but I decided instead to include the power of the students' collective work on standards and acceptability. The effect on Johnny's mother was immediate. She was impressed not only by the standards themselves but also with the evidence of quality student work around the room. The real message, however, was in the quality of Johnny's work when considered against the rather impressive classroom "evidence." Of course, not all students have the same capabilities. But *all* students must have high expectations held for them. Johnny fell short and in the end his mother knew it. More importantly, Johnny knew it.

Is this story unusual? Perhaps the fact that students were asked about standards and quality is unusual. Don't students know when their efforts are of quality? There are always instances of self-delusion among students, but when push comes to shove, they know when their efforts are deserving and when they are wanting. Johnny Brosz was no exception. He probably had been allowed to get away with shoddy work over the years to the point where it was fine with him.

## Expectations and Standards

Why would a teacher even accept a piece of work for assessment when on a first scan it is clearly not acceptable? It is logical that if a teacher takes in work that is of poor quality; spends time reading, assessing, and marking it; and then hands it back to a student, albeit with a very low assessment, then poor quality work is acceptable! Johnny Brosz, fortunately, encountered a teacher who was prepared to avoid this trap. There was no suggestion that student work, when judged to be unacceptable, be handed back without comment, advice, or counsel. Clearly, professionalism dictates that teachers provide guidelines for young people and suggest ways their learning might be more successful. Students know what is solid effort and what is not. The results can be quite amazing when they have an authentic voice in determining the criteria for solid effort and holding themselves accountable.

Discussions that describe schooling using terms such as *caring, humanness, student voice, student involvement, liberation, honor and respect for young people, student-teacher response journals, relationships,* and *defining young people* are sometimes dismissed by critics as being *soft*. This somewhat disparaging term is meant to relegate such discussions to the realms of the wishy-washy, weak, and ineffectual. The problems with today's youth, this argument often goes, is that they are not dealt with strictly enough. "This is what you have to do; do it, or face the consequences!" Back-to-basics proponents revel in this position. The "this is what you have to do" implication demands more nose-to-the-grindstone drill and practice, where memorization and regurgitation would be valued for their short-term demonstrations of academic gain.

Paradoxically, however, this logic is likely the perpetrator of many of the ills that pervade society and schooling. In a time of unparalleled change, when many of the stabilizing institutions in society are crumbling, young people need the skills and competencies to know how to help themselves. "This is what you have to do; do it, or face the consequences" is a stance that clearly breeds dependency. Johnny Brosz was in many ways a victim of this dependency. He was used to being told what to do. Unfortunately, he was patterned to produce inadequate work and get away with it.

## Self-directedness

In today's complex and changing times young people need the skills and competencies to be self-directed. They need these abilities in caring, inviting, and human learning environments where altruism and rigor coexist. Skills should be explicit within a curriculum framework. The "softness" criticism is unfortunate and ill-founded. High expectations would be essential to help young people in an academic, intellectual way, as well as in affective, social-emotional ways. Noddings (1992), strongly promotes an "ethic of care" in schools and rejects the anti-intellectual criticism. "My position is not anti-intellectual. It is a matter of setting priorities. Intellectual development is important, but it cannot be the first priority of schools" (p. 10).

If young people are to be successful in today's world, they must understand that the essence of success in this complex society is about altruism. Industry wants intelligent, thoughtful team players who work well with colleagues. Society generally wants intelligent, thoughtful citizens, who are socially aware and care for the people and institutions of that society. Most of the difficulties society is experiencing concern the inability of people to get along and work together. The instant gratification and passivity engendered by some technologies and the persuasiveness of commercialism, produces in people generally and young people particularly, a sort of lethargy and reluctance to engage in the kind of quality that demands rigor. The Johnnys of this world have been used to minimal standards. He was neither motivated nor expected to do anything better than what he was doing—merely handing something in. **To what extent does curriculum exert control over and encourage dependency in young people?** When this is the case, is it any wonder that students possess little ability to direct their lives? Johnny was lucky he met a teacher who wasn't prepared to do all the work for him. He was invited to establish the conditions for learning and then to live by them. Should he choose not to abide by the conditions, there would be no confrontation. Johnny's work was simply not accepted. So, what are you going to do about it, Johnny Brosz?

# Rigor

Rigor, in the true sense of the word, cannot be imposed. By definition, *rigor* is the strict interpretation and application of rules and expectations. In authoritarian and autocratic societies and institutions the imposition of the rules and expectations would be by fiat. Young people do not learn to become enlightened and self-directed in these environments. In democratic societies and institutions, people must learn to *become* responsible, competent, and caring. Young people cannot learn these qualities unless they are permitted to experience opportunities to be responsible, competent, and caring.

Rigor, in these circumstances, would indeed be present through the demands of high expectations for learning. The fundamental difference between authoritarian and democratic places is that of profound respect for the value of the individual and the collective voice in community affairs. Yes, rules can be laid down, consequences declared, and foreboding manifestos produced, but rigor in learning will only come about through motivation. A teacher can insist on notebooks of a certain quality and appearance, on formats and deadlines, and on rules for behavior. All this is laudable and necessary. True rigor, rigor that produces a richness in learning, will only come about through a curriculum in which young people have a voice, where the learning has connections to life, and where some real control of the learning is with the students. Teachers who have planned for, or observed, students working in these ways will know vividly of what we speak. It is this rigor, coupled with the active involvement of students in determining standards and expectations, that evokes excitement and quality. Consider some examples of this learning at work:

- High school students on the first day of classes in September sitting down with their teacher considering the course goals and objectives laid down in the program of studies from their district.

  TEACHER:    Here's what we are expected to do. Let's consider these statements and decide what they mean.

  STUDENTS:    [General conversation and questions about word meanings. Clarification of meaning and understanding.]

  TEACHER:    Okay. How would you like to go about learning these requirements? Let's start to plan the year.

- Primary school teacher wants to build curriculum around the needs and interests of her children. She asks the children to write down how they feel about school and what they like doing.

  GINNY:    "I like school alot. I like swimming, horses, and reading. I have two brothers and three sisters. I am glad I am in your room and we are going to have so much fun in this room."

PAUL: "I hope I will like this school and I have a sistre thats in school rite mioe [now] and shes in grade 5. and I like going to my frands House. I all so like dinosros and I go to 7 e ll [7-11] to play games and I like it to.

AARON: "I leve ate [acting] I haf win mie mem an sest [sister] an bog cat an brt [bird] mi fafrt [favorite] suplac [subject] is art dramu musie I hp [hope] we hef a gut hre [year]."

Teacher uses this data to begin conversations about what to learn and how the learning will take place. Expectation become a natural part of the talk.

- Group work in junior high social studies.

    TEACHER: Now that we have some understanding of the things we have to do about history, let's consider how we might go about it. Let's start off with how you enjoy learning best. Who wants to start?

    STUDENT: I like to work with other people, but I don't like too many in my group.

    STUDENT: I like working with other people but not all the time. I think you should take the whole class a good bit of the time, Mrs. Blackwell.

## Student Voice in Curriculum

There can be no denying the power of voice and the accompanying ownership. Of course students can't take over curriculum planning. Teachers must guide and often direct the process. The three previous examples embrace student voice with the teacher as guide. Student voice, in these examples, does not compromise the high expectations that characterize rigor in a curriculum. In any endeavor we are understanding, with increasing clarity, the need to serve the "client" first. In business the message is clear: Those who serve the client most effectively prosper. The others falter or fail because the clients will go elsewhere. In schools our "clients" are captive and for the most part unable to go anywhere else—physically, at any rate. But mentally? The difficulty we have engaging students in learning is a form of absence. The kinds of curriculum that students must experience contain subjects that have few connections to their lives, let alone to each other. They are determined by committees, or professional bureaucrats, for faceless youngsters. Largely because they are young, young people are not consulted. It is another example of the arrogance of authority. In any endeavor, those who know if the shoe fits are the ones who must wear the shoe. **Why are young people seldom consulted about the "whats" and the "hows" of their learning?**

A few years ago a random sample of 60 ninth-graders was brought together for a day to talk about schools, learning, and teachers. Their conversations were rich, honest, and animated. Summarizing and synthesizing their talk was not easy, but it was possible to identify key statements related to five areas of interest:

1. relationships
2. teachers
3. variety
4. time
5. voice

This was not a scientific study, but any time young people are together to talk seriously about their learning and their lives in school, adults would be wise to listen. Consider these key, collective responses to each expressed area of interest, along with some explanatory comments gleaned from the conversations:

**1. We like working with other students when we are given the chance to cooperate and show leadership.** Young teen-agers like to cooperate with others in their learning. At this age, relationships are important to the success of their learning. Typically, students indicated the following:

- Friends' reactions helped them to learn more about themselves.
- Learning was more enjoyable when they worked with people with whom they felt comfortable.
- Working with others helped them to improve their social skills.

Their discussion about cooperation in learning focused on group work. They believed that group work should involve everyone, use people's strengths, and involve learning related to their world. Leadership opportunities provided by group work enabled young teen-agers to understand and engage in peer helping, peer teaching, and self-teaching.

**2. We like teachers who are knowledgeable, respectful, friendly, and can relate to us.** Young teen-agers appreciate helpful and encouraging teachers who are interested in what is being learned, know their subjects, and actively model what they expect of students. Teachers who hold clear and high expectations are valued.

Treating people equally and with respect is very important; no stereotyping and double standards. There is strong appreciation for teachers who are sensitive, considerate, and accepting of young people as they are. Relationships characterized by friendliness, fun, and humor are sought and valued. The most effective teachers are those who can relate to young people and, in this regard, the most essential qualities are sincerity and trust.

**3.   We are more successful when we have variety in what we learn and how we learn it.** Young teen-agers want greater variety in ways of learning and teaching. Hands-on learning experiences are particularly important. There is a desire for a wider range of learning resources. Learning styles are acknowledged with the request that they be reflected in learning opportunities. There is concern when what they are being asked to learn is seldom connected to life out of school. They want to demonstrate their learning in a variety of ways. Clearly teen-agers see learning as more than texts, paper, and pens.

**4.   We like being able to decide how we will use our time.** Young teen-agers want greater flexibility in nearly every facet of their learning. When discussing their classes, they express a need for more time to talk, ask questions, share thoughts, and determine their own time limits. In a more general sense, they want opportunities to manage their own time and to experience more individualized study periods. They believe class time is not necessary for everyone.

**5.   Teachers help us to learn best when they let us have a say in our learning.** Young teen-agers desire some control over their learning. While they acknowledge the central role of the teacher, they want to share in decisions about their learning. Specifically, they are concerned about what they are learning, how it is to be learned, and the time they devote to learning. Many believe that what they are being asked to learn is neither meaningful nor connected to their lives. They mention frequently the need to learn things in school that help them to be more successful out of school. Also, they want to be active participants in learning that is guided by their real questions and where mistakes are considered part of the learning process. It is very important that adequate time be provided to develop skills and apply what they have learned.

This accounting of time spent with ninth graders provides strong support to our discussion of the need for a "lived" curriculum. Anything that is lived has life at the center. A lived curriculum must have connections to the lives of those for whom the curriculum is intended. In the five statements gleaned from conversations with young people, it is clear they were not asking for learning that was easy or without challenge. Rather they were seeking "rigor that produces a richness in learning . . . through a curriculum in which the young person has voice" (p. 106). Instead of controlling, directing, and imposing curriculum on young people, learning would be greatly enhanced by inviting, collaborating, and sharing, so that they would lend the curriculum their lives. To do this we are again drawn to the wisdom of the seventh-grade girl who simply, yet profoundly, asks teachers to "move over a little." When teachers "move over," not only will the curriculum live, but young people will become more alive.

≈ THROUGHOUT THE GEOGRAPHY OF NORTH AMERICA UNIT students had been quizzed orally and in written form on their conceptual understandings. Multiple choice, true-false, and fill-in-the-blank assessment techniques had been used to determine what skills and content knowledge had been learned to date. To complement these assessment tools, teachers used reflective journals, informal conferences, and performance demonstrations to help develop a picture of what had been learned.

As a team we believed strongly that the type of assessment used should fit with the type of learning that had been taking place. There were times when facts and memorized pieces of information were deemed to be important and therefore an appropriate assessment tool was selected. There were also times when students were given a framework of the skills and competencies covered to date and were asked to demonstrate their understanding by a means of their choice. Some students made trifold presentations, others conducted interviews and did library research, and others elected to set up a debate looking at social issues confronting North Americans. The range of demonstrations was as diverse as the students themselves.

The Geography of North America unit concluded with an overall assessment of the unit itself. Students were given a questionnaire that not only asked what significant types of learning had occurred during the unit but also what suggestions they might have if this unit were to be taught again.

The team of teachers in this story used a variety of assessment techniques. They understood that a multiple-choice test does not give a complete picture of what a student understands. It simply provides one piece of the assessment puzzle. Our earlier story about whole-school curriculum raised questions about fragmentation, connectedness, and meaning in relation to curriculum. It is important to realize that these three areas are of equal concern when it comes to the assessment of curriculum. **How can we make assessment a lived experience so it is alive and has meaning?**

## Authentic Assessment

Our story emphasizes the need for assessment to be congruent with significant instructional goals. Cognitive learning theory and its constructivist approach to teaching and learning supports the need to integrate assessment methodologies with curriculum content. The role of assessment should be to provide authentic and meaningful feedback for improving teaching and learning. Assessment methods are useful and productive to the extent that they represent significant outcomes for students and the instructional goals of the classroom. In other words, to be valid, fair, and useful, the assessment strategy selected must match the knowledge, skills, and attributes that the teachers are teaching and those that the students are expected to learn. Ergo, there must be a positive and direct correlation between assessment and curriculum.

In the previous story teachers "believed strongly that the type of assessment used should fit with the type of learning that had been taking place." Clearly there is no one right way to assess students. Performance demonstrations may give an indication of how well students can apply their knowledge, where multiple-choice tests may be more efficient for determining how well students have acquired a set body of knowledge. A balanced curriculum, which for example requires students to synthesize, organize, and memorize, requires a balanced approach to assessment.

New visions of teaching, learning, and curriculum delivery, such as the "KWL" approach, demand attention to broad-based assessment. Learning is no longer thought to be a one way transmission of knowledge, from teacher to student. Learning must actively engage students. Good teachers draw on subject knowledge, student-lived experiences, and learning theory. As such, a variety of instructional strategies are employed to meet the variety of learning styles found in a classroom.

Chapter 4 discussed Gardner's notion of multiple intelligences. When we consider assessment it is important to realize that to be successful with all students, teaching, learning, and assessment needs to draw on more than the linguistic or logical-mathematical intelligences. **What are the implications for assessment of Gardner's multiple intelligences?** If assessment is an integral part of teaching and learning, then shouldn't consideration of curriculum outcomes be the first step in designing meaningful assessment tasks?

The first step in assessment design, or selection, as with curriculum development, is to know the purpose of your assessment. In our story the teachers seemed to know and were able to articulate their curricular outcomes. Students were given a framework of the skills and competencies covered in the unit. Good assessment demands this type of attention to outcomes. It is these explicit outcomes, be they knowledge- or process-based, that determine the aspects of performance that are the subject of the assessment. That is, what do you want your students to be able to do, or demonstrate, at the end of a unit or course? The answer to this question should define the learning and teaching activities inherent in a given unit, as well as the assessment employed. Also, rigor, in these circumstances, would indeed be present through high expectations for learning. Such a fit among teaching, learning, and assessment would allow for a more comprehensive picture of student achievement and a clearer indication of a curriculum's effectiveness, as well as determine the degree to which a curriculum was truly lived.

# An Invitation to the Reader

The following page suggests a process for thinking about the chapter, to stimulate conversation, encourage debate, share stories, provoke further questions, challenge current thinking, or engage in further personal reflection. University classes, professional development groups, school staffs, and parent groups may find the chapter's questions and related text useful, as a challenge to personal beliefs, understandings and experiences, toward affirmation or change.

We present the concept of "filter." Readers are invited to consider the central question of the chapter, along with the questions that arise from the text. It is not our intention to limit or reduce context to one small portion of the chapter—we are conscious of the problem of reductionism. It is our hope that, as readers proceed through the book, they will respond to questions in a more holistic manner.

The concept of filter is a metaphor for the reader's personal beliefs, values, and experiences, through which new ideas are explored and current beliefs challenged. It is this filtering that provides an opportunity for the reader to make personal connections to the questions and ideas in the chapter. This process may provide an opportunity to deepen meaning and understanding of the concepts and ideas discussed.

**In the following framework, you are invited to contemplate your beliefs, understandings, and experiences through reflecting on the questions and related text in Chapter 5.**

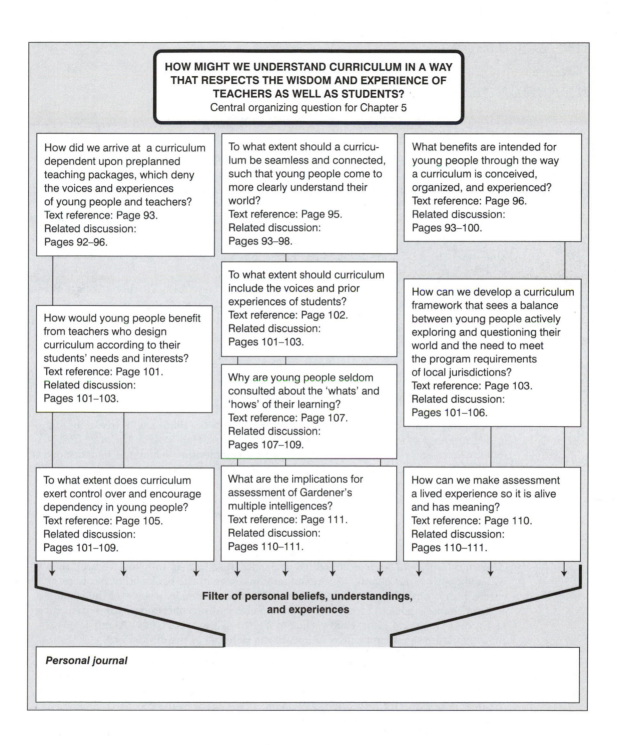

**HOW MIGHT WE UNDERSTAND CURRICULUM IN A WAY THAT RESPECTS THE WISDOM AND EXPERIENCE OF TEACHERS AS WELL AS STUDENTS?**
Central organizing question for Chapter 5

How did we arrive at a curriculum dependent upon preplanned teaching packages, which deny the voices and experiences of young people and teachers?
Text reference: Page 93.
Related discussion: Pages 92–96.

To what extent should a curriculum be seamless and connected, such that young people come to more clearly understand their world?
Text reference: Page 95.
Related discussion: Pages 93–98.

What benefits are intended for young people through the way a curriculum is conceived, organized, and experienced?
Text reference: Page 96.
Related discussion: Pages 93–100.

How would young people benefit from teachers who design curriculum according to their students' needs and interests?
Text reference: Page 101.
Related discussion: Pages 101–103.

To what extent should curriculum include the voices and prior experiences of students?
Text reference: Page 102.
Related discussion: Pages 101–103.

How can we develop a curriculum framework that sees a balance between young people actively exploring and questioning their world and the need to meet the program requirements of local jurisdictions?
Text reference: Page 103.
Related discussion: Pages 101–106.

Why are young people seldom consulted about the 'whats' and 'hows' of their learning?
Text reference: Page 107.
Related discussion: Pages 107–109.

To what extent does curriculum exert control over and encourage dependency in young people?
Text reference: Page 105.
Related discussion: Pages 101–109.

What are the implications for assessment of Gardener's multiple intelligences?
Text reference: Page 111.
Related discussion: Pages 110–111.

How can we make assessment a lived experience so it is alive and has meaning?
Text reference: Page 110.
Related discussion: Pages 110–111.

**Filter of personal beliefs, understandings, and experiences**

*Personal journal*

## REFERENCES

Aoki, T. (1991*). Inspiriting the Curriculum and Pedagogy: Talks to Teachers.* Edmonton, Alberta: University of Alberta Press.

British National Commission of Education. (1993). *Learning to succeed.* London: Heinemann.

Costa, A. et al. (Eds.). (1992). *If minds matter: A foreword to the future.* (Vol. 1) Palatine, IL: Skylight Publishing, Inc.

Greene, M. (1971). Curriculum and Consciousness. *Teachers' College Record, 73*(2), 253–269.

Moffett, J. (1994*). The universal schoolhouse: Spiritual awakening through education.* San Francisco: Jossey-Bass.

Noddings, N. (1992). *The challenge to care in schools.* New York: Teacher's College Press.

Taylor, F. (1911). *The principles of scientific management.* New York: W. W. Norton and Co.

## SUGGESTED READINGS

Readers may find a book by MAUREEN MCCANN MILETTA (1996) useful in expanding understandings of student voice in curriculum matters. Her book, *A Multiage Classroom: Choice and Possibility*, describes how three elementary school teachers decided to relax the compartmentalization of learning into subject areas and shuffle subject matter into new patterns to offer students a voice in their education. The newly designed learning environment was a place where learning was valued, where students had choice in what they learned, and where teachers were at liberty to develop imaginative programs.

The 1995 Yearbook of the Association for Supervision and Curriculum Development, *Toward a Coherent Curriculum,* edited by JAMES BEANE, is an informative book that will add depth to our chapter. A fundamental message in the book is that a coherent curriculum is one with parts that are unified and connected by a sense of the whole. Sixteen chapters cover a broad perspective on curriculum coherency, with writers such as ERNEST BOYER, MARION BRADY, GRANT WIGGINS, MAXINNE GREENE, and JAMES BEANE making significant contributions to the richness of the discussion.

Our views on schooling would support the design of curriculum for diverse learners. In this regard an interesting article by ALICE UDVARI-SOLNER and JACQUELINE S. THOUSAND (1996, May) titled, "Creating a Responsive Curriculum for Inclusive Schools," (*Remedial and Special Education,* v17 n3 pp. 182–192) presents reconstructionism as a useful way to design curriculum in inclusive schools. The writers propose theoretical foundations and the use of learner-centered, process-oriented, and communication-based instructional approaches as promising practices in curriculum design for diverse learners.

# 6

# CREATING AN INVITING SCHOOL

## AN INVITATION . . .

Our concluding chapter invites the reader to reflect on the conditions in schools, the ways of working we create to do that which needs to be done. We take the position that it is not uncommon to find hierarchical approaches to school organization in which teachers and students tend to be controlled in ways that silence their voices. Hierarchical structures often isolate teachers and limit opportunities for meaningful talk about learning, teaching, and curriculum. The deeper understandings and intentions of curriculum tend not to receive adequate attention. The discussion takes the position that schools must be designed for work in ways that encourage ongoing, continuous learning.

**What conditions would encourage meaningful participation of students and teachers in leadership and decision-making toward individual and school growth?**

Creativity, interest, and motivation are all enhanced when individuals know their voice is valued. We believe that a school organized around democratic principles would encourage collaborative decision making, shared leadership, and a sense of ownership by all. The final section of the chapter proposes that a school demonstrating these principles would see leadership as a moral enterprise; a learning community characterized by an ethic of caring.

⪢ BROOKSIDE SCHOOL WAS GETTING TOO BIG. The principal, Mrs. Gross, had been reading literature that suggested that arrangements of "schools-within-schools" were useful for creating smaller groupings of students. She liked this idea. She thought it would be good for developing closer relationships between staff and students. If, say, the school's 400 students were divided into four "schools," each with a fixed number of teachers, they could operate as small communities, a bit like organizational families. Mrs. Gross intended to create an atmosphere of smallness where the benefits could be realized through better results on tests and all-around improved success in learning.

At the next staff meeting she explained her intentions to the staff. Her introductory remarks were written out so that she would not forget important ideas. "I would like to finish the business section of today's staff meeting early so that I might explain some of my intentions for our school. I have some exciting ideas to share with you. I am going to give you the chance to discuss the ideas so that you have opportunity for input. Here's what I plan for our school. . . . " So began Mrs. Gross' schools-within-a-school journey.

In the days after the meeting, staff-room and hallway talk was active. "What harebrained idea is this?" said one veteran teacher.

"She didn't go to a conference, did she?" groaned another.

Julie Smith, a second-year teacher, was enthusiastic. "You know, we talked about this in our university classes. I think it sounds exciting." The aging staff, however, was generally unenthusiastic. Mrs. Gross, having no way of tapping into this hallway talk, pushed ahead with administrative zeal.

The Christmas holidays passed and Mrs. Gross was ready with her new administrative plans. Students were grouped, teachers assigned, and the timetable reorganized. She had an exciting holiday creating the new arrangements.

Spring break arrived and the staff was on its knees. The flurry of committee work was seen by staff as an increasing imposition. Perhaps the most glaring omission was the lack of attention to a revised curriculum design. What Mrs. Gross intended was not how the school was turning out. She felt as though she was fighting a losing battle. Could she stand another term like this one?

As May drew to a close and plans for next year were being discussed, staff slowly but firmly began to express their feelings. One veteran teacher, who had known Mrs. Gross for some time, dropped into her office and alerted her to the general feelings of staff. "You know, Rosemary, you don't have a happy group of campers out there." The picture was vividly painted. At future staff meetings, others ventured their opinions until, eventually, Mrs. Gross had to face reality. What she had almost evangelically intended, was neither understood nor shared by her staff. Time to regroup and take note of other literature that deals with ownership!

---

**M**rs. Gross committed the cardinal sin of single-mindedness. Her very well intentioned pursuit of improvement for her school was ignoring a fundamental tenet of organizational effectiveness—working with and through the people who must make the new organization function. Clearly, Mrs. Gross was a fine person. She was concerned about her students. She wanted the best possible relationships between staff and students. No doubt she understood that successful learning is founded on effective student–teacher relationships. However, new organizational arrangements, which depend on a staff for their effectiveness, must involve that staff in their design, conceptualization, and implementation. New ways of working demand new ways of thinking and new ways of thinking do not occur through legislation. We are reminded here of our discussions of change in Chapter 2, where the emphasis on *things* as opposed to *people* was questioned. Could it be that Mrs. Gross was so consumed with her new way of organizing (the thing) that she gave little or no attention to those who must make the new organization work (the people)?

## INTENTIONALITY IN SCHOOLS

The matter of intention looms large. Mrs. Gross was motivated solely by *her* intentions. Because she was the instigator of her intentions, she was left with the task of selling them to her staff and then, because of the rapidity of her actions, trying to make people implement the organization with all the necessary enthusiasm. The ensuing problems resulted from people who had (1) little or no commitment to the initiative, (2) little or no ownership in the initiative, (3) little or no time to explore the new meanings and understandings of learning and teaching required by the initiative, and (4) no ownership in the initiative. In short, Mrs. Gross was trying to impose a new organizational arrangement on a conventional setting. The fundamental flaw was the assumption that because it was new and presented by administration with enthusiasm, people would embrace it with equal enthusiasm.

Intention is a powerful concept. In law the proving of intention may be the difference between guilty and not guilty. In cases of murder, the proving of intention is the difference between first degree and second degree murder, with all that the difference entails. In an organizational context, intention is a powerful and primary consideration in establishing focus and direction. Schools tend to establish their "purpose." Statements of purpose describe what a school considers itself to be about. As primary organizers for improvement processes, these statements tend to lack definition and attention to the point that they may inadvertently contribute to the very thing they are designed to avoid—stagnation and a "stuck" condition (Rosenholz, 1989).

To explicate this matter further consider the definition of the term *intention:* determination to act in a certain way. If we understand this in an organizational context, then literally the people who make up an organization would act with this required determination. Clearly, to act with determination requires that people accept and understand what is required by the intentions. At Brookside school, Rosemary Gross was comfortable acting according to her intentions. Her staff, on the other hand, neither accepted nor understood those intentions. In other words, the intentions were not those of the school, only those of the principal. Had Mrs. Gross persisted, she would have had to rely on the power of her position to make staff embrace her new organizational arrangement. This tendency to tell and make people do things in our learning environments (see Chapters 2 and 4) is endemic. It is also a major impediment to change.

## Spheres of Intention

Schools need to pay attention to that which needs to be done, to achieve "a deep understanding of the most important things that ought to be done" and then make sure that "they are done effectively" (Low, 1993). If we revisit the definition of *intention* and consider the most important things that ought to be done to break the constraints of convention, four spheres of intention emerge:

1. fundamental
2. essential

3. program

4. technical

Figure 6.1 presents a more detailed explanation of intentions.

**FIGURE 6.1**
Curriculum Intentions

**Fundamental Intentions**

Understandings of the central purpose of school:
- The abilities of young people to fathom and competently respond to the problems, issues, conventions, and protocol of the wider culture.
- The generative learning abilities that enable young people to be contributing members of society and lifelong learners.
- The personal decision-making skills and competencies that provide young people with confident, self-directing qualities.
- A school culture with degrees of socialization that embody altruism, compassion, and justice, toward a global spirituality.

**What needs to be done?**

**Essential Intentions**

Quality and equity in learning opportunities for all young people:
- Opportunities for equal access to knowledge for all students.
- Invitations to learn that respect people as human beings.
- Learning that accepts teachers and students as co-learners within the context of the social construction of knowledge and meaning.
- Learning environments that offer a moral context that promotes personal ownership.
- Learning that provides young people with an active voice in decisions and opportunities to experience authentic responsibility.

**What needs to be done?**

**Program Intentions**

Learning opportunities that support personal aspirations:
- Program offerings that enable post-secondary admission.
- High, but reasonable, learning expectations for all young people within all learning opportunities.
- A variety of program offerings to embrace the expressed interests of students.
- Connections among learning that focus on life-related topics of relevance to students.
- Links with the world of work that create awareness among students.
- Athletic and recreational programs accessible to all students.

**What needs to be done?**

**Technical Intentions**

Management and organizational activities:
- Communication with constituents.
- School policies and procedures.
- Schedules: staff/parent/school council meetings/school timetable
- School governance

**What needs to be done?**

The **fundamental** sphere concerns the broad intention of a school. It responds to the statement: "At the end of a young persons experience in this school they will be able to.... " The fundamental intention is held for all young people without regard for ability or subject area. The **essential** sphere is equally important and concerns itself with learning. It requires a school to be clear about its understanding and orientation toward learning for all young people. These understandings are in effect throughout the school learning environment. The intention applies to social learning and academic learning equally. Lunchrooms, hallways, and playgrounds would be considered equally as important as classrooms. The **program** intentions concern themselves with the programmed learning experiences planned by the school. These intentions describe the kinds of experiences young people will have as they progress to becoming more competent, caring people, more contented members of their peer group, and more contributing members of society. It is through these intentions that a school embeds the first and second sphere intentions into an operational plan, such that the curriculum is bound into a coherent whole, truly endowing all the parts of the curriculum with meaning.

> Being concerned with the whole does not mean a mere adding together of facts from the various specialized disciplines. Such facts become relevant only when interpreted in terms of a frame of reference that can encompass them and give form and shape to a conception of the whole. It is not likely that such a conception will arise from research that is simply interdisciplinary in the usual sense of the word— that is, involving the cooperation of several interdisciplinary specialists. For knowledge of society as a whole involves not merely the acquisition of useful insights from neighboring disciplines, but transcending disciplinary boundaries altogether. (Bellah et al., 1985, p. 300)

The **technical** intentions describe the management practices of a school. Taking direction from the preceding spheres of intention the technical intentions operationalize matters. In essence, the technical intentions establish the conditions for doing that which needs to be done. Use of time, for example, would be a critical case in point. The true determination to act in facilitating ways would be put to a real test within the technical intentions.

Intention spheres represent an extension beyond the expressions of conventional mission and purpose statement activity. Typically, statements of mission and purpose concern themselves with the program and technical intention spheres, with perhaps some gesture toward essential intentions. Mrs. Gross was firmly mired in the technical sphere, with some deference to program intentions. It is most important that the spheres of intention are understood through the question, "What needs to be done?" A determination to act in a certain way would reap benefits to a school community. Through determination toward action, conditions are established. Conditions are organizational arrangements, based on knowledge and understandings of human learning, that enable a school to do that which needs to be done. They generate collective response which allows a school to do, with coherency, that which needs to be done. Brookside school lacked the collective response for coherency of action. Mrs. Gross laid down organizational arrangements clearly enough, but the conditions did not enable *the school* to act with coherency, because the conditions were not based on knowledge and understandings of human learning. Staff members were not invited to consider and reflect on new knowledge, toward new understandings of learning, teaching, and organizational thought.

## An Orbit of Responses to Intentions

Between any organization moving from its intentions to its general well-being there exists an orbit of responses. This orbit is so called because it requires a constant movement through the different activities. When an organization's intentions are clear, when there is clarity about that which needs to be done, there immediately exists a tension among three needs in the organization.

1. the need for action
2. the need for meaning and understanding
3. the need for prerequisite skills and abilities

Our penchant for pragmatism in schooling is often an impediment to progress and change. We fail to allow people to attend to meaning and understanding associated with new concepts and practices. Also, we tend not to ascertain whether people possess the necessary skills and abilities to effectively implement changes. Certainly an organization needs to get on with business. It is unrealistic to expect people to spend all their precious time sitting around talking about new ideas. However, rushing into practice with undue haste is fraught with pitfalls, many of which are amply documented in a review of change initiatives in schools over the last 15 years or more. Figure 6.2 summarizes our discussion of an organization's intentions and the three needs of the people working toward that organization's well-being.

The need for action, to get on with things, must be accompanied by reflective activity. People must be constantly seeking meaning and understanding associated with the innovative activity. They engage in social constructivist behavior, to understand new concepts while concomitantly telling the truth about their collective professional reality with regard to skills and abilities. **How often, in schooling, do we assume we possess the skills and abilities to implement new conceptual frameworks for learning and teaching, when we may have only limited experience with their application?** If Mrs. Gross' unhappy "group of campers" were being honest with themselves, a good portion of their discontent would have been with their general inability to work in the ways demanded by her "schools-within-a-school" initiative. All facets of the schema are important for a well-intentioned school.

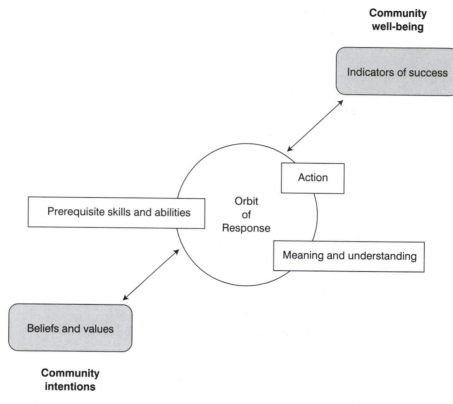

**Figure 6.2**
Organizational Intentions and Needs

If intentions are unclear, then no matter how strong the determination to act, a school will likely fall prey to the aphorism that looks at a group of people with ill-defined directions and suggests that unsure of where they were going, they redoubled their efforts. Without clear, collectively determined intentions, schools may well find that efforts lead to neither personal nor organizational well-being. **To what extent should ownership be part of a school's vision and intention?**

❧ WESTSIDE SCHOOL HAD BEEN OPERATING in traditional ways for as long as people could remember. The school district was starting a requirement for school improvement. Each school was to design a continuous school improvement process, based on current knowledge about learning, teaching, and organizational thought. A young staff member, Arlene, had moved to the district's

Curricular Services Unit and through her relationships with the principal and staff, she was to be their resource person.

"How do we get these people off their butts to start talking about new knowledge?" This rather colloquial beginning launched the first discussion between Arlene and the principal. Needless to say, the opening remark was attributable to Arlene. The principal, feeling the pressure from the district, encouraged the conversation and eventually other teachers were invited to be part of the discussion.

"What we need," Arlene said, "is to have a staff meeting and ask the staff about their main areas of concern."

"I think you'll need more time than a regular staff meeting will allow," said a teacher.

"What about our next professional day?" inquired another.

"Excellent idea," said the principal. "Nothing's firmed up yet for that day."

"Arlene, will you design a process for us and facilitate the day?" The school was off and walking.

Arlene planned a day focused on learning and activities to determine the staff's main areas of concern about the school. The underlying idea was to set up conditions for the school to decide what it wanted to do to improve. Basing its work on the mornings discussions of learning, the hope was that the conditions for improvement would see the staff dealing with the identified areas of concern.

It is important to understand that the school was attempting to design a framework for improvement, organized around areas of concern to the staff, and including the expectation that staff would learn new ways of behaving. In short, it was to be a continuous school improvement plan based on understandings of human learning. The teachers divided into four goal groups, with a representative from each goal group who would meet with the principal and Arlene to act as a steering committee.

The various committees began to meet and plans began to emerge. Each goal group developed lists of things to be done and the steering committee facilitated communication. Some of the difficulties, of which the school increasingly became aware, centered on the lack of time available for the entire staff to deal with the work of the goal groups. They found that perhaps only two or three whole staff meetings were available, per year, for a particular goal group's work. Implications for the continuous learning of the school began to surface.

Arlene began to worry about the real implications of human learning. "Is learning based in the completion of things to be done?" she asked herself. After all, that's really what the goal groups have done to this point. "Maybe the framework we've designed to manage the improvement process is getting in the way of human learning."

New knowledge in the world is increasing at an exponential rate. New knowledge in the field of education is no exception. Organizations require ways of becoming informed about and understanding this constant avalanche of new knowledge. Westside School had a group of staff members who were gaining exposure to new knowledge through their learning and teaching goal group activity. The rest of the staff members, however, were engaged in other things. The lack of time for them to deal with the work of the learning and teaching goal group was problematic. Within the organizational scheme of things, learning and teaching—the very essence of a school's existence—was relegated to equal importance with three other more peripheral activities. It is not sufficient to say that people should take it upon themselves to read professional literature.

## VALUING HUMAN LEARNING

Increasingly, it is necessary for organizations to see themselves as communities in which learning is a fundamental part of the ways work is done. In short, organizations—or the people who make up the organization—must be designed to work in ways that encourage continuous learning to occur. A thorough knowledge of human learning is needed. How would this apply to Arlene and Westside School?

For an organization to function differently, the people who make up that organization must learn to see their world differently. Learning is not the mere acquisition of facts, or the taking in of information. For true learning to occur human beings must experience a shift or movement of mind.

> Real learning gets to the heart of what it means to be human. Through learning we recreate ourselves. Through learning we become able to do something we never were able to do. Through learning we re-perceive the world and our relationship to it. Through learning we extend our capacity to create, to be part of the generative process of life. (Senge, 1990, pp. 13–14)

The intentions discussed previously call for a kind of collective vision, a set of moral commitments that transcend the special interests of individuals or groups toward the welfare and prosperity of all young people in a school. It is what Sarason (1986) would call a triadic connection, a confluence of the individual, collective, and moral responsibilities:

> A guiding vision that reinforces a bond between the sense of 'I' and the sense of "we," a kind of meeting ground where the nature of the vision is under constant scrutiny and discussion and informs proposals [and conditions] for action. (p. 904)

The essential morality of the schooling enterprise demands learning in community, true learning with a genuine shift or movement of mind. Ultimately it is the individual who will learn, but human learning is a social experience.

# Collective Learning

It is crucial to organizational growth and improvement that conditions facilitate people coming together to discuss the central intentions of the organization. Working collectively, people need to gain clarity in understanding what the organization is about. Organizational charts, diagrams, descriptive prose, and other promotional literature will not effect human learning. Individuals engage in collective learning toward their personal contribution to the collective moral purpose; the growth and prosperity of the young human beings who are the school's raison d'etre, or reason for being. As people in schools move from their intentions, into their day-to-day work with students and with each other, their activities should reflect learning in process.

It is useful to consider Westside School's efforts at continuous school improvement. Were their intentions clearly understood? The story simply recounts the creation of four goal groups, each paying attention to a facet of school life. Each goal group developed lists of things to be done and the steering committee facilitated communication. Consider the following list of things to be done taken from Westside's documents:

### Goal Group: Learning/Teaching Goals
- Maintain or exceed the 1993–94 percentage of students achieving the acceptable standard of performance.
- Work toward all students completing courses.
- Assess the effectiveness of our programs in meeting student needs.
- Assess the congruence between our programs and our achievement goals.

### Practices
- Monitor placement of students at the commencement of each course.
- Examine school policy with regards to student transfer of courses/retroactive credits.
- Establish a process whereby students complete courses.
- Begin a process for tracking identified special needs students.
- Reassess the practice of accepting students as special placement.
- Examine and, as required, alter our programs to meet the needs of our students

We do not wish to be unfairly critical of Westside School, in its honest attempts to effect change. We simply offer the excerpt for question and reflection. What kinds of change would likely occur as a result of Westside's declared goals and practices? If these declarations are intended to contribute to continuous school improvement, then what specifically is to be improved? The Goal Group in question is concerned with learning/teaching. How will learning and teaching benefit from continuous improvement? Clearly this scenario contains unknowns. We do not know how the school is developing its improvement process, but we do have their beginning statements and the history of schooling to call on for our indicators. Organizations do not tend to change unless the people who make up the organization experience shifts, or movements, of mind. Individuals must learn to see and experience their world differently.

We wonder if Arlene and her colleagues were pursuing that shift toward a collective moral purpose? A common response to improvement is often to tinker with management practices. In our spheres of intention this would involve mostly the technical intentions with some attention to the program intentions. The real attention to learning, to defining young people differently, to understanding learning as a profoundly human and social experience, to defining curriculum through life-related experience and through understandings of young people responding to their world, in self-directing and contributing ways, seems absent. Westside appears to have embarked on a convention-bound journey, to seek a mere variation to the management of schooling.

Consider the following piece of information, generated by another school, to improve school effectiveness.

### Action Group: Instructional Emphasis Goals
- Clarify and set academic expectations of students.
- Involve students in setting course objectives.
- Orient homework toward success.
- All students master basic course content.
- Students establish a positive attitude toward homework
- Students make effective use of class time.
- Correlate the amount of homework within each organizational "pod."
- Pay more attention to the higher-level mental activities.

### Practices
- With students, plan the emphasis and timeline of course objectives and content.
- Each organizational "pod" will discuss and correlate the distribution of homework each week.
- Work that is expected of students will tax their use of time.
- Spend time asking higher-level questions.
- Use varying assignments and "pod" remediation to ensure that skills are mastered and that brighter students remain challenged.
- Homework will be marked and returned as promised.
- Students accurately complete their homework.

Do you notice any significant differences between Westside's work and the second sample? Of interest is the time span separating the two pieces of work. Westside is active at the time of writing. The second sample was completed in 1980! This rather feeble attempt at drama is intended only to raise questions. What have we been doing all these years? Shouldn't there be a change in the ways we approach schooling? Where is the evidence of the incredible amount of new knowledge available to us during the past 15 years? If human learning was not prominent in organizational development knowledge in 1980, then surely the wealth of knowledge accumulated since then should be evident today.

Westside pays no attention to intentions of the fundamental or essential kinds. The profound questioning of the ways of knowing in schools and the reasons behind them seems to be absent. The clinical list provided by Westside seems like a mechanical litany of things to be checked off as they are completed. Westside's list raises questions about assumptions, or mental models, discussed in Chapters 1 and 4. If the sole purpose is to implement the activities, then without concomitant attention to changed understandings, brought about through attention to human learning, the teaching staff would likely be bringing conventional assumptions, or mental models, to their practice. Without attention to meaning and understanding associated with new concepts about learning, teaching and organizational thought, even if their goals and practices implied new ways of working, no change or improvement of any significance would likely occur.

We have on a number of occasions referenced historical practice. On a previous page we quote an example from 1980. These forays into history are intended to make the point that schooling does not seem to *learn* from its knowledge base. If a school considered a curriculum framework such as the one presented in Chapter 5 (p. 96) then perhaps changed understandings would be encouraged. If fundamental and essential intentions were explored, then different approaches to learning and curriculum might emerge. Once again the question of learning within an organizational context is paramount. **If human learning is essentially a social experience, if new knowledge and meaning are socially constructed, then how should this be reflected in our understanding of schools as communities?**

## Toward Learning in Community

Senge (1994) suggests organizations that establish conditions that facilitate continuous learning are in fact learning organizations. *Communities of learners* is perhaps a better term but, whatever one's preference, such a place constitutes the following:

> An organization where people continually expand their capacity to create the results they truly desire, where new and expansive patterns of thinking are nur-

tured, where collective aspiration is set free, and where people are continually learning how to learn together. (Senge, 1994, p. 3)

In schools, where pragmatism is so dominant, the conditions for continually learning how to learn together are often absent. Use of time, such a precious commodity, is dedicated to management items. Organizational patterns, focused on conventional uses of time, leave little opportunities for staffs to attend to anything other than management-type matters. This is the paradox of convention. Conventional uses of time see teachers busy with their individual timetables. Any times when teachers come together are consumed with school management matters (testing schedules, report cards, calendar items, extracurricular events, special days, discipline, public relations needs, district office demands, governments mandates . . . the list is endless). Dealing with new knowledge becomes almost incidental, if it happens at all.

Arlene and her colleagues at Westside School seemed to be adopting a management approach to their school improvement planning: What can we do differently? The organizational rearrangement they adopted was quite seductive. It could be illustrated, published, and duly communicated, giving the impression that great things were happening. Again we revisit our "things" versus "people" question. Is the school really effecting a change in the things they do, when really their real concern should be in the new meanings and understandings that the people are bringing to their work? Would the people at Westside be able to continually expand their capacity to create the results they truly desire, where new and expansive patterns of thinking are nurtured? It is doubtful, without new patterns of working together, where teachers could shape their days, where teachers could discuss their practice, in conditions where the social nature of human learning would be respected and where the social construction of new knowledge and meaning would be honored. We believe that schools need to establish conditions that encourage the meaningful participation of students and teachers in leadership and decision making toward individual and school growth.

∾ MY PRINCIPAL CALLED ME INTO HIS OFFICE and began to talk about my learning community's approach to teaching and learning. During our conversation he indicated that a system-based consultant was interested in meeting with our teaching team to discuss our program for the upcoming year. The consultant was interested in discussing such issues as curriculum design, authentic assessment, and student voice and choice. To be honest my first reaction was, "Oh great, yet another nonschool-based expert who will come into our meeting and tell us how we should do things." My past experiences had led me to believe that consultants provided the theoretical hows and whys during meetings and then disappeared.

Well, much to my surprise, this consultant was different. Dylan Waldo came to our meeting accompanied by the principal, introduced himself, and provided us with an overview of his background and experiences. At the end of the meeting he asked our team for permission to meet with us regularly throughout the school year.

During the first few meetings he contributed what at first I thought to be little in the way of substance. He sat back, listened, recorded a few notes, and asked a few questions. His questions were nonthreatening and seemed to always draw our team back to our beliefs and values. It was clear that our team was becoming comfortable with Dylan as his ideas began to simply become part of our discussion.

Our timetable allowed us to meet as a team for an hour a day. Each meeting was used for a specific purpose. For example, we would talk about students, curriculum, reflection, deal with administrivia, and plan. On Tuesdays we discussed curriculum and Mr. Waldo agreed to meet with us every Tuesday for the entire year. This in itself was a commitment we were not used to getting from system-based personnel.

During one meeting centering on thematic curriculum, Dylan indicated his excitement for our plan by expressing his desire to roll up his sleeves and work as part of a teaching team. There seemed to be a need on his part to understand the context and experiences that shaped our—and ultimately his—work. As a result of this experience I think his ways of working with teaching teams can benefit both teachers and students.

---

The school organization provided teachers with an opportunity to talk daily. Within the traditional management structures of schools it may be argued that opportunities for teachers, let alone teams of teachers, to sit down and talk on a regular basis is nonexistent. If we believe that it is important to develop fundamental and essential intentions, then the organization of the school must provide the conditions to make it happen. Once the conditions are in place, teachers must then be pragmatic in terms of time usage. The teachers in the story had an hour a day allotted as preparation time. The team made a conscious decision to identify needs and specifically designate the purpose of each preparation time. In the life of a teacher there is always something else to do that takes precedence over using time to discuss teaching and learning.

The routine technical tasks of teaching such as photocopying, laminating, cutting, pasting, or lesson planning, are most often done in isolation, by individual teachers. How often have teachers been heard to lament, "We just do not have time to sit around and talk, there is too much to be done!" How might we organize and use time differently in schools to facilitate inquiry into learning and teaching? Literature is full of articles inviting people to think in systemic ways, build learning organizations, work as teams, and think collaboratively. Yet in schools we seem to have difficulty seeing that the things we do are steeped in conventional ways of thinking. We attempt to interpret current experiences using old models and metaphors that are no longer appropriate or useful. Schools must move away from simply taking an idea (the thing) and forcing its implementation without considering fundamental and essential intentions. The teacher in our story initially thought Dylan Waldo would come into the team meeting and control the direction and decisions, by playing the role of outside expert. The conditions in place allowed the team of teachers and the consultant to meet regularly and continually. The traditional tendency for a consultant to be a "one-shot wonder" was removed and instead a relationship was formed in which he simply became another member of the team. **What type of organizational configuration would facilitate ongoing opportunities for teachers to talk about teaching and learning?**

❧ MARTHA PILKINGTON HAD BEEN TEACHING FOR 30 YEARS. She was a kind person. Her life was devoted to her work, her invalid mother, and her piano. Technically, she was a wonderful pianist. Teaching also was a technical job for her. Worksheets were her stock in trade, with one exception. In language arts, her second-grade children worked from phonics workbooks. Mrs. Pilkington considered phonics the solution to the literacy problems befalling children today. "Children do not know how to attack words and that is why they don't know how to read. Too much television." In her day children were taught to read by breaking words into syllabic sounds and learned to read with little difficulty. Dick and Jane prospered.

Janet's classroom was across the hall. She was a lively, young teacher in her fourth year at the school teaching third grade. Janet, still fresh from university and a disciple of James Britten, almost evangelically espoused the whole-language approach. Martha and Janet did not see eye-to-eye on how to teach children to read. According to Martha, Janet was destroying the solid foundation the children had been provided in second grade. "You cannot be creative without the skills. How could you possibly deal with a piece of student writing without marking the student errors?" After 30 years of teaching, Martha figured she had learned something about teaching students to read.

The case of Martha and Janet is typical of many conflicts in schooling. The reluctance to understand approaches to learning and teaching, in the context of accumulated knowledge, is often an impediment to progressive discussion at teacher professional development sessions. Janet's youthful zeal and Martha's unyielding entrenchment contributed to a stuck school. Openness and reflective practice, both necessary conditions for continuous improvement, were significantly impeded by the intransigent attitude of these two teachers. The reality in many schools is that inflexibility and relative rigidity in the use of time and resources, makes the infiltration of contemporary thinking into the pedagogy of learning and teaching environments more complicated.

Dylan Waldo, in a previous story, tried to engage the teachers in reflective thinking about their work with young people. He was attempting to establish what Sizer (1984) would call a sense of "honest dissatisfaction" with the learning, teaching, and general ways of organizing for learning in schools. Dylan knew that "telling" a group of teachers was a recipe for rejection. Teachers need an invitation to reflect in a supportive, collaborative setting on their ways of responding to the learning needs of young people. Martha and Janet needed similar invitations. The key difference between the work of Dylan and Martha and Janet's school was the organizational conditions. The teachers working with Dylan had common time to meet, each week, to reflect on their practice and plan accordingly. Martha and Janet worked in isolation, in closed classrooms, with little or no opportunity to work collaboratively. The organizational conditions for Martha and Janet denied the implementation of current knowledge about human learning and change.

Schools might usefully try to avoid becoming simply institutions of rhetoric, embracing the trend and attendant language of the times (collaboration, teaming, shared decision making, and so on) as the thing to do, and give more attention to understanding meaning. In Chapter 2 we discussed the need for people to develop meaning and understanding. The things that are implemented must emanate from deep understandings of the learning needs of young people. To gain this understanding it is necessary to have clarity about the learning needs of teachers. Unless human learning is the primary reference point for what we do and how we design our learning environments, how can we hope to move teachers from rhetoric to reality? **What conditions exist in schools to help facilitate human learning?**

It seems possible that Dylan Waldo's questions, which brought the team back to their beliefs and values, may be one way of peeling away the layers covering the assumptions and beliefs at the heart of our work, which ultimately may lead to an honest questioning of what we do and why. The goal groups at Westside School did not seem to be based on knowledge about how people learn. The goal group meetings were divorced from students. The teachers went back to their separate classrooms to make decisions. What was it about Dylan's way of working with a team of teachers that caused them to have a different experience? Was his way of working based on knowledge about human learning? We know learning to be, primarily, a social experience. We learn by talking to, listening to, working with, and watching others. The goal groups at Westside provided sporadic and restricted opportunities for teachers to interact. The team of teachers in our story met every day for an hour. On Tuesdays they met with Dylan, who raised issues and questions that caused the team of teachers to wrestle with their central, fundamental intentions. There is little doubt that these continual, ongoing interactions, helped the teachers develop meaning, as they formed their intentions, in a collective and collaborative manner. **To what extent do our school learning environments recognize that human learning is a social experience and therefore provide teachers with an opportunity to talk about learning?** Human learning also requires opportunities for reflection. The events, occurrences, and experiences in one's life need to be processed to give meaning for one to learn. **What conditions exist in schools to allow for reflection on and in practice?**

---

❧ *REFLECTIVE PRACTICE* AND *COLLABORATION* weren't part of my language when I was in my student teaching year. Looking back, I can now identify what we were doing as collaboration and reflective practice. My cooperating teacher, Miriam West, was a wonderful woman and teacher. We spent three months in the classroom together discussing, writing, planning, observing, and team teaching. We constantly asked questions and learned from one another. We soon became friends. Laughter and chatter intermingled with our work. It was a caring and exciting place to go each day.

With the student teaching experience behind me, I began my first year of teaching in a new school. I got my timetable (which included a subject I had never taught) and my classroom and was sent on my way. I made it through the first week or two with the feeling that I was coping, but something was missing. Who could I talk to about my ideas for units, how a lesson went, and the stories of some students? Who would respond to my journal writing? Sure, there were teachers down the hallway that I talked to between classes and before and after school, but these conversations seemed superficial in comparison to the ones with Miriam. I learned to tolerate my isolation that year, but I never stopped missing and searching for that close relationship with a colleague.

In my second year, the school underwent some changes and teachers were organized into team-teaching groups. Kevin Miller was my partner in working with about 50 students. Almost as soon as we began, I was reminded of my work with Miriam. Once again, I found myself in a rich relationship with another teacher. It was during this experience that I was introduced to the language of collaboration and reflective practice. I could finally identify what I once had, then lost, and regained, hopefully never to lose.

---

Why is it that in most schools, relationships are not nurtured once we have graduated from teacher education programs? It seems that independence, self-sufficiency, and individualism are deeply entrenched and fiercely protected in schools. Unfortunately, these norms inhibit collaboration, the sharing of stories, and reflective practice among teachers. What are we missing by living our lives as teachers in isolated settings? Clearly, the beginning teacher in the story believed she was missing something important to her growth and experience as a teacher.

## Collaboration, Shared Stories, and Reflection

What strikes us most about the individualism and isolation that characterizes work in most schools is that it isn't congruent with current knowledge about human learning. The social construction of knowledge requires dialogue and sharing of ideas and experiences among two or more people. For meaningful learning to occur, consistent and ongoing conversations and sharing need to take place. Collaborative relationships based on reciprocity, respect, trust, shared purpose, and dialogue (LaRocque & Downie, 1993) take time to develop. The nurturing of collaborative relationships requires time and places for talk, as part of the regular rhythm of the school day. The time and place for the relationship to grow was built into the teacher education program in our story, but what regular, ongoing times and places are there for teachers in schools to engage in this type of collaborative learning? The lack of attention to collaboration in most schools seems to imply that professional learning is finished after the teacher graduates from student teaching.

What might happen if we began to value the type of collaborative relationships and learning environments often developed in teacher education? Suppose schools were organized so that times and places for teachers to work and learn together were provided. Clandinin (1993) describes the beginning of collaborative relationships:

> We began to know our own stories better by hearing others' stories. As we listened to others' stories, we not only heard echoes of our own stories, but saw new shades of meaning in them. . . . We learned to make spaces for each other in which to hear our voices, to know that in our voices were our ways of making sense of our selves and our work. (p. 2)

As we share our stories with one another we find new meanings and deeper understandings of ourselves and our work. The sharing of stories, in this way, would be a way of making schools places where learning for teachers is valued. Clandinin (1993) further reports on Sherri, a student teacher, and Deb, the cooperating teacher, who write to one another in a journal:

### Sherri

At the university I was learning to listen to the children's stories, to listen and value their stories as being part of who they are. One afternoon I saw Andrea crying her eyes out at her desk. At first she blurted out her frustration about the glue on her artwork not sticking. As I listened to what she had to say, the meaning of her tears became clearer. Andrea's parents are divorced and it was her birthday on Saturday. She really wanted to have a party, but she usually spent the weekends with her dad. This dilemma was creating considerable stress for her. I too had grown up in a family torn by divorce and constantly spent weekends away from my friends. I shared this story with Andrea. We talked together about how it felt. She was no longer crying when our conversation ended. Later in the afternoon I mentioned the talk Andrea and I had shared. Such an important story! It was eye-opening for both of us. It reminded Deb to listen to the students' stories for the meaning they convey, and I made a connection between what I had been taught at the university and the realities of the classroom.

### Deb

For me, now, learning to listen to students' stories is becoming an important part of my practice. The more I know about their stories the more I understand about them.

I sat with Kamil's mom at parent-teacher interviews. I expressed some concerns about Kamil's inability to sit still and attend to his work for any length of time. In tears, she told me the story of their escape to the mountains, in Iran, three years ago. She told me of the frightening and struggling going on in their country. She said Kamil was only three years old at the time but that he has vivid memories of this horrifying experience. Kamil's mom wants him to be in a place where he is loved and where he knows she is loved. I look at Kamil differently now. Children's stories are so important. We need to know who they are so that learning can take place.

We had no idea, through sharing a classroom, we would be sharing an experience that would begin to lead us inward, to question ourselves and why we do what we do. As we struggle with this discovery, we are learning who we are as individuals and teachers. We are on this road of discovery together. The occasions are endless. We have shared, talked, laughed, and hugged our way to knowing. We know ourselves better and we know the students better. Our relationship, as a team of learners, grew from our stories. (pp. 26–27)

Through shared stories, journal reflections, and team-teaching, Deb and Sherri, like the teachers in our story, were able to build a strong collaborative relationship. They were learning and had shared intentions. **How could we create environments in schools that invite reflective practice?** We believe that consideration should be given to new ways for designing school learning environments that encourage collaboration, learning, and caring among teachers. Perhaps team-teaching arrangements, like the one in the story that included the beginning teacher and Kevin Miller, is one way of inviting teachers to work and learn together.

More important, though, is not the design we might employ to create such inviting environments, but that teachers in a school have a valued voice in making decisions about intentions and improvements related to the design. Without this voice and participation, a change, no matter how well-intentioned, would be difficult to implement. Incorporating voices and designing appropriate learning environments immediately raises questions of leadership. What kinds of leadership would motivate people to design and nurture learning places where their voices are respected, valued and actively embraced in the day-to-day learning?

## LEADERSHIP

It is important that conditions and the ways of governance in a school be based on intentions and human learning. Schools often talk about voice, choice, and student-centeredness as the things to do, but are they seductions based on a current trend? Schlecty (1990) would offer caution about actions based solely on "truth, beauty and justice, as opposed to effectiveness toward desired results" (p. 51). A school's intentions should emanate from beliefs and values about human learning and leadership. Shared, collaborative leadership would be aimed at fostering such learning.

◣ IT WAS THE START OF A NEW SCHOOL YEAR, and with it came extracurricular and committee sign up time. "Who would like to coach volleyball or basketball, be a member of the professional development committee, or sponsor the Student Council?" Student Council had always been an interest of mine, so I put my name on the list. I was one of five teacher sponsors, and as a group we decided to get together to plan the year's council. We began by discussing how the council should be run and what the organizational structure might look like. One teacher finally said, "It seems crazy that we, as teachers, are even having this conversation. This is a council for students, so why the hell are we making all the decisions?"

We looked at each other in amazement and almost in unison said, "You're right, where are the students?"

Needless to say teacher planning stopped and we brought together a sampling of our student body to discuss their council. One interesting notion arose, as often does when students are provided opportunities to speak. Suzie, one of our more outspoken students, thought that Student Council should be more than a group that runs dances and organizes food drives. She thought it should play a role in all schoolwide issues and policies. Suzie was aghast by the number of decisions that were made in the school without the students being allowed a voice. Much conversation ensued between staff and students and as a result a school governance committee emerged.

Were the intentions of the school clear, in the minds of the teachers, as they began to organize the Student Council?

## Voices of Students

We wonder if the past student councils alluded to in our story were simply management techniques, used to give the illusion that students played a significant role in the school's day-to-day activities. If our intention is to effect authentic responsibility and involvement on the part of our students, then are they part of the conditions for governance? The student in our story was "aghast by the number of decisions that were made in the school without the students being allowed a voice." Does this comment apply to many of our schools? If so, is it not in direct contradiction with what a democracy stands for? We live in a democratic society, yet our schools do not reflect such ideals. The teachers in most schools represent 5% to 10% of the population, yet make 95% to 100% of the decisions. **What role should students play in the governance of a school?**

Many schools claim to develop responsible students who should take ownership for their learning. If this is truly a fundamental intention, then how is it reflected in governance of the school? **To what extent do students have authentic experiences that genuinely validate their voices in school life?**

Our story reminds us of the importance of voice in learning. Britzman (1990) helps us to come to a deeper understanding of voice with her view that:

> Voice is the meaning that resides in the individual and enables that individual to participate in a community. . . . The struggle for voice begins when a person attempts to communicate meaning to someone else. Finding the words, speaking for oneself, and feeling heard by others are all a part of this process. . . . Voice suggests relationships; the individual's relationship to the meaning of his/her experience and hence to language, and the individual's relationship to the other, since understanding is a social process. (p. 14)

Her explanation connects voice to human learning as a social process. In our story, Suzie was finding her voice, speaking for herself and being heard. In the ensuing conversation the group came to an understanding, thus highlighting the relationships and social process involved in voice. The teachers in the story came close to silencing the voice of Suzie and the other students, by not including them in the initial dialogues. Suzie and the other Student Council members would have lost the opportunity, then, to struggle for their voices, communicate meaning to others, and come to understandings together. They would have lost an opportunity to learn. **In what ways do we silence the voices of young people?**

## Voices of Teachers

Our story focused on the involvement of students in their schools. Through sharing this story, we were able to question the intentions of schools with regard to student involvement and governance. We also found an important connection to voice and learning. What about the voice of teachers? Many schools claim to be places where shared decision making and collaboration is the norm. **How often are the voices of teachers heard in ways that contribute to pedagogical meanings and understandings that influence the school?** Clearly, there are legitimate questions to be raised about school leadership and opportunities created for the voices of teachers and students in the determination of intentions and directions for a school.

---

🍃  JACK CHALMERS JUNIOR HIGH WAS A NEW SCHOOL, so new in fact, that when school was due to open in September, the place wasn't even finished. We all assembled anyway and trooped into our first staff meeting with the new principal. Albert Jackson was an affable man, even when he wasn't smiling he seemed to be. He got the first staff meeting off to a good start, emphasizing relationships and staff getting to know one another. Soon the students would be here and the year would be under way.

Albert Jackson was unobtrusive, yet he knew everything that was going on. As a teacher into my sixth year of teaching I was past the "rookie" period where much of the time is learning the ropes. I was feeling settled and beginning to seriously consider career aspirations. Some kind of administrative position was in my plans and I watched Jackson closely to see what I could learn. There were four things I observed about him which, as I have pondered over the years, have been quite powerful to my career: First, he was always in the building. Second, he actively encouraged people to try new ideas. Third, he spent a lot of time developing relationships. Fourth, he was firm in his expectations and would not tolerate shoddy professionalism.

Whenever classes changed he was in the hallways. When students were dispersing before school, at lunchtime, and after school, he was always standing in the same place greeting them, exchanging banter, and generally getting to know them. The students referred to him affectionately as "Uncle Albert."

Any teacher wanting to try something new, for which money, permission, or moral support was required, found a great ally in Albert. Yes, he would want to discuss the matter, but the discussion was to be informed so that he could support the initiative in whatever way was necessary. I remember dealing with labor relations in my ninth-grade social studies class. Collective bargaining was the topic and our class scenario was enacting a labor dispute. This called for a strike by one group of students and pickets were parading around the school, with signs visibly displayed. Well, Albert's phone lit up with concerned members of the community. He enjoyed every minute of it. He knew what was going on and relished each explanation. I felt empowered to take on the world.

Albert was wonderful around the staff room, too. Always there for lunch, or to stop by for a brief chat at other times. He shared stories about his family. He opened his home for staff parties. He was first to call if any staff member was ill. We all considered Albert our friend.

But he was no pushover. Let any staff member take liberties with students and see what would happen. Let any staff member display incompetence in the classroom and Albert would be there with very clear intent. He held clear expectations and standards for himself and for his staff.

Albert Jackson was also democratic. Staff members were invited to establish policy and practice for the school. Philosophy and curriculum were constant agenda items and even though some staff meetings were monotonously long, few could argue that voices were not heard. Albert was not the most informed leader I have met, but he was an effective and influential one.

---

Albert worked from disposition and intuition based on a sound traditional view of good teaching. His grounding in current knowledge about learning and learning community design was questionable. He was an efficient manager and possessed wonderful social skills. And he cared about kids. Albert ran what Sergiovanni (1984) would have called a good competent school. He managed his school, his staff, and his parents well. To what extent was he a leader?

Leadership has been and continues to be a vexing, elusive topic in education. Our literature is replete with theories and some research espousing the merits of this or that approach to administrative leadership. Clearly there is no one style of leadership for promotion over others. To a considerable extent a good leader acts from disposition and intuition, based upon knowledge of learning, teaching, and learning community design.

## Leadership and Management

Caution needs to be exercised here lest we lapse into unproductive semantics. Leadership and management, as practice, are not discrete. However, some questions of substance need to be addressed, the responses to which might provide insight into matters of progress, change, and general enhanced success in learning, in our increasingly criticized approaches to schooling. Our position is that the questions concern matters of attitudes and assumptions. Leadership and management may be seen as orientations. The extent to which we dwell in the management orientation is the extent to which we may succumb to rhetoric, as a response for leadership. Similarly, the extent of leadership dwelling might more likely describe an orientation with attitudes and assumptions disposed toward working with and through people, to seek a successful route to follow. Of course, this is not an either–or matter. People do not exist exclusively in one or the other orientation, but the attitudes and assumptions displayed quite naturally declare a certain disposition. It is this disposition toward a certain orientation that is germane. Think about Albert again. A wonderful person, but in what ways was he leading his school? What indications in the story provided suggestions about focus and direction for his school?

Management, in a strict interpretation, is looking after the business at hand and getting things done in the most efficient ways possible. It is not unusual for efficiency to be rewarded and acknowledged as leadership. Consider Figure 6.3 and the attitudes and assumptions representative of an extreme management orientation. Schools are, of necessity, pragmatic places. When young people are not present, teachers engage in stimulating conversations, where the theories and ideas of scholars and thinkers in the educational universe are considered, challenged, embraced, and debated. When students reappear the next day and classes commence, an ambience of pragmatism tends to pervade the enterprise and managing becomes dominant.

| Management/Administration Behaviors | Attitudes | Assumption |
|---|---|---|
| Hierarchical organizational structure | Authority and control are needed for a "well run ship." | The power of authority can affect success in school. |
| Control in all aspects of an enterprise | Presence is necessary to know what is going on and to ensure it is going on well. | Subordinates cannot be trusted to get things done on their own. |
| Task completion | A manager's/administrator's primary role is to get things done. | Efficiency is essential for a successful learning environment. |
| Interpersonal relationships | Recognizing conformity. All for the team…right or wrong. Dissent is not dignified. | Contrary opinions constitute negativity and are not tolerated. |
| Management of successful learning | If learning experiences are allocated adequate time and resources, and teachers manage their time well, then students will learn successfully. | Time, resources, and well-organized classes will result in successful learning. |

**FIGURE 6.3**
Typical Characteristics of Management/Administration Orientation

This vexing phenomenon is at the root of the lack of success that schooling has experienced with enacting change. Teachers must cope with the organizational circumstances to which they are assigned. These circumstances often demand pragmatism solely as a way of coping—coping with large classes, dealing with specific time blocks in which to manage learning, making sure the curriculum is covered, marking student work in sufficient quantity to be able to establish a grade score, fitting in supervision and extracurricular responsibilities, and so on. Teachers have little control over their in-school lives. The quest for efficiency is marked by control. The presence of control is exercised through power, and power denies liberation. Unless teachers are liberated to harness their collective wisdom, experience, and professional knowledge, and to apply their insights toward the greater success of the schools in which they work, then schooling is unlikely to benefit from enduring progress and change. What is required in our school systems is profound leadership that does not deny the need for critical inquiry before action begins. Such leadership would establish the conditions for teachers to engage in real collaboration, so that they might work together—not in isolation—to effect the most successful learning for all students.

Figure 6.4 provides comment on the salient features of a leadership orientation. The two figures describing the two orientations may be expressed as a continuum (see following diagram). Looking at the leadership/management question this way allows us to consider our discussions in a particular context. It would be interesting to think about Albert Jackson in this way. Where would Albert fall on such a continuum?

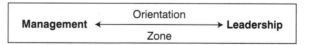

Semantics must always be a constant caution in discussions such as this, but it is important enough to pursue with some tenacity. Our position, throughout this book, has pointed to the constraints of conventional schooling in the pursuit of change. We have strongly advocated for caring, human, learning environments where meaning and understanding of current knowledge about young people, learning, teaching, and learning community design, determine what needs to be done in our schools. Ownership, we have argued, is paramount for all constituents. Power and control must be devolved so that students and teachers, according to rigorous standards and expectations, might work as co-learners toward their greater prosperity. The leadership needed to create these kinds of conditions is profound. Johnson and Johnson (1989) hold the following:

> Leadership begins where management ends, where the systems of rewards and punishment, control and scrutiny, give way to innovation, individual character and the courage of convictions. (p. 1:4)

| Leadership Behaviors | Attitudes | Assumption |
|---|---|---|
| Facilitate organization | Devolution of authority and control to teachers in matters to do with learning and teaching. | Teachers have the collective wisdom to know how best to organize to meet student learning needs. |
| Shared decision-making / shared responsibility / shared leadership | Trust in the competence, integrity, and professionalism of teachers. | Teachers can be trusted to know what needs to be done. |
| Actions determined on their contribution to meeting students' learning needs | Decisions based on the degree to which student learning needs are positively affected. | Successful learning is based on understandings from contemporary knowledge. |
| Interpersonal relationships | Recognizing importance of developing relationships. Works with and through the strengths and passions of staff. | Dissent is dignified. Diverse views are valuable. |
| Nurtures communities of learners in a spirit of critical inquiry | Learning is an individual experience which cannot be exactly predicted. Learning time and organization must be flexible. | People learn in different ways and at different rates. |

**FIGURE 6.4**
Typical Characteristics of a Leadership Orientation

Albert Jackson certainly would have fallen short on innovation. He supported individual teachers in their pursuit of new ideas, but there was never a sense of contribution to school direction and focus. It was almost as though some sort of osmosis would occur. Almost as though the encouragement of individuals to do new things would somehow benefit all. There was no sense of orchestration, no sense of contribution to the common weal, no declared intentions. Teachers working in isolation, doing interesting things, are still working in isolation. Whether the students benefited was inadvertent at best.

The focus and personal ownership of a school's intentions and direction must be a primary purpose of leadership. Sergiovanni (1992) considers leadership to be moral and personal. He would urge us to question the "management mystique" which has tended to describe our approach to leadership. This is consistent with our position, but it is his moral and personal comment we choose to emphasize. Teaching and schooling are both profoundly moral. Adults are intervening in the lives of young people and, as such, must do so through invitation and with humility. Power, control, and the sticks of authority cannot be countenanced in schools. Our leadership must invite, inspire, and accompany young people in their learning, in their process of becoming. Freire, expressing views on empowerment, encourages school leaders "to think less about administrative efficiency and more about student learning, instructional facilitation, and long-term change" (Timpson, 1988, pp. 63–64). It is the move away from a management orientation that is germane.

In Chapter 3 we shared a story about Freire and his meeting with a reporter from *OMNI* magazine. The behavior of Freire in that story is an example of his people-focused orientation. The leadership disposition we espouse rejects control and places a considerable emphasis on understanding people. Relationships based on caring, empathy, compassion, and trust are directed toward transformational behaviors at the personal and institutional levels. The struggle to transform is marked by humility and a lack of judgment. The transformation is toward changing schools into places where intentions and conditions are focused on the fostering of human learning. Relationships can be easily misunderstood. Those who approach relationship development from a professional point of view may well fall prey to solely congenial and convivial behaviors. These high-profile behaviors are often marked by a certain superficiality, which calls into question the motives behind their purpose. Social activities, contrived get-togethers, end-of-the-day wine-and-cheese sessions, "secret buddy" schemes, and other similar group-focused practices tend to be orchestrated to the point of being artificial. They may be described as management-designed, professional climate building experiences. Personal relationships are profound. They demand a certain sharing of one's self so that distance between people is reduced. Personal relationships are based on people and not on role. Leadership required to establish a school culture of trust, ownership, caring, and genuine collaboration would certainly have a strong element of professional relationships, but the strength of the personal relationships would measure the strength of the school. Fullan (1992) sees this kind of leadership as being focused on changing the culture of the school:

> They build visions, develop norms of collegiality and continuous improvement, share strategies for coping with problems and resolving conflicts, encourage teacher development as career-long inquiry and learning, and restructure the school to foster continuous development.
>
> These leaders develop collaborative work cultures that raise individual and group commitment and capacity, thereby providing a powerful environment for assessing instructional practices and for making improvements on an on-going basis. (p. 7)

## Ownership and a Moral Commitment

Transformation toward a school culture that is owned by the people who make up that culture would be a primary leadership goal. Clearly ownership cannot be mandated. Management practices marked by control and power would produce superficial results at best. What is needed is leadership behaviors where people are empowered, trusted, and supported in the devolution of control, responsibility, and accountability.

Fullan (1992) speaks of the need for people to experience a deepening of ownership as they engage in transforming a school culture. People do not always readily embrace ownership. Because of our long history of convention-bound schools dominated by management behaviors, many people are still of the "tell me what you want me to do" mentality. It is the leadership skills of working persistently with and through people, toward enhanced personal and institutional learning, that leads to success. The persistence in divesting the school of hierarchical power positions is a vexingly complex matter. It is not only complex for leaders themselves, but exacerbated by the protocols of a convention-bound institution. The complexity and pervasiveness of the problem is underscored by Sarason (1992), who advises that "the school and school system generally are not comprehensible unless you flush out the power relationships that inform and control the behavior of everyone in these settings" (p. 7). The changing of our school cultures, then, requires powerful and profound leadership. The power relationships to which Sarason refers are among teachers and administrators, parents and school staffs, students and teachers, schools and their districts, and other agencies with responsibilities for schooling. The rather daunting task of leadership to effect cultural change, to flush out the power relationships, might benefit from Fullan's (1990) reflections on change and five assumptions of which he believes a leader would be wise to be mindful.

1. Assume that any significant innovation, if it is to result in change, requires individual implementers to work out their own meaning.
2. Assume that people need pressure to change (even in directions they desire). But it will only be effective under conditions that allow them to react, to form their own position, to interact with other implementers, to obtain the technical assistance, and so on.
3. Assume that changing the culture of institutions is the real agenda, not implementing single innovations.
4. Assume that no amount of knowledge will ever make it totally clear what action should be taken.
5. Assume that you will need a plan that is based on the above assumptions. (Fullan, 1990, p. 2)

The advice contained in Fullan's assumptions brings to mind once again Albert Jackson and his life at Jack Chalmers Junior High School. Individual meaning was not a priority at the school. Individuals could pursue innovation, if they wished and Albert would likely give them maximum support. Albert would really have Fullan's assumption reversed: Implementing single innovations is the real agenda, not changing the culture of the institution. The leadership required to effect the rigor and humanity in learning, which we have shared in this book, is profoundly moral. Schools must change. They must change to keep pace with the world in which they exist. More important, they must adapt to help young people better understand themselves and their world, a world that is becoming more complex by the day. If we truly care we will, together, pursue the deepest possible ownership of our learning and the schools in which young people are served.

## AN INVITATION TO THE READER

The following page suggests a process for thinking about the chapter, to stimulate conversation, encourage debate, share stories, provoke further questions, challenge current thinking, or engage in further personal reflection. University classes, professional development groups, school staffs, and parent groups may find the chapter's questions and related text useful, as a challenge to personal beliefs, understandings and experiences, toward affirmation or change.

We present the concept of "filter." Readers are invited to consider the central question of the chapter, along with the questions that arise from the text. It is not our intention to limit or reduce context to one small portion of the chapter—we are conscious of the problem of reductionism. It is our hope that, as readers proceed through the book, they will respond to questions in a more holistic manner.

The concept of filter is a metaphor for the reader's personal beliefs, values, and experiences, through which new ideas are explored and current beliefs challenged. It is this filtering that provides an opportunity for the reader to make personal connections to the questions and ideas in the chapter. This process may provide an opportunity to deepen meaning and understanding of the concepts and ideas discussed.

**In the following framework, you are invited to contemplate your beliefs, understandings, and experiences through reflecting on the questions and related text in Chapter 6.**

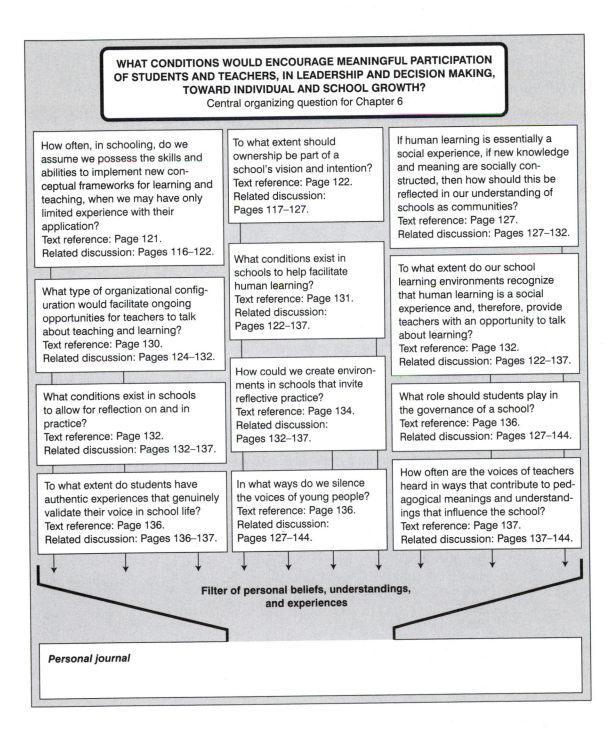

**WHAT CONDITIONS WOULD ENCOURAGE MEANINGFUL PARTICIPATION OF STUDENTS AND TEACHERS, IN LEADERSHIP AND DECISION MAKING, TOWARD INDIVIDUAL AND SCHOOL GROWTH?**
Central organizing question for Chapter 6

How often, in schooling, do we assume we possess the skills and abilities to implement new conceptual frameworks for learning and teaching, when we may have only limited experience with their application?
Text reference: Page 121.
Related discussion: Pages 116–122.

To what extent should ownership be part of a school's vision and intention?
Text reference: Page 122.
Related discussion: Pages 117–127.

If human learning is essentially a social experience, if new knowledge and meaning are socially constructed, then how should this be reflected in our understanding of schools as communities?
Text reference: Page 127.
Related discussion: Pages 127–132.

What type of organizational configuration would facilitate ongoing opportunities for teachers to talk about teaching and learning?
Text reference: Page 130.
Related discussion: Pages 124–132.

What conditions exist in schools to help facilitate human learning?
Text reference: Page 131.
Related discussion: Pages 122–137.

To what extent do our school learning environments recognize that human learning is a social experience and, therefore, provide teachers with an opportunity to talk about learning?
Text reference: Page 132.
Related discussion: Pages 122–137.

What conditions exist in schools to allow for reflection on and in practice?
Text reference: Page 132.
Related discussion: Pages 132–137.

How could we create environments in schools that invite reflective practice?
Text reference: Page 134.
Related discussion: Pages 132–137.

What role should students play in the governance of a school?
Text reference: Page 136.
Related discussion: Pages 127–144.

To what extent do students have authentic experiences that genuinely validate their voice in school life?
Text reference: Page 136.
Related discussion: Pages 136–137.

In what ways do we silence the voices of young people?
Text reference: Page 136.
Related discussion: Pages 127–144.

How often are the voices of teachers heard in ways that contribute to pedagogical meanings and understandings that influence the school?
Text reference: Page 137.
Related discussion: Pages 137–144.

**Filter of personal beliefs, understandings, and experiences**

*Personal journal*

# REFERENCES

Bellah, R. N. et al. (1985). *Habits of the heart: Individualism and commitment in American life*. New York: Harper & Row.

Britzman, D. (1990). *Practice makes practice: A critical study of learning to teach*. New York: Suny Press.

Clandinin, D. J. (1993). *Learning to teach, teaching to learn*. New York: Teachers College Press.

Timpson, W. M. (1988). Paulo Freire: Advocate of literacy through liberation. *Educational Leadership, 45*(5), 62–66.

Fullan, M. (1990). *Assumptions about change*. A one-page document distributed at Association for Supervision and Curriculum Development Mini Conference, Educational Change—Imperative for the Nineties. New York, March 1992.

Fullan, M. (1992). The concept of transformational leadership—A brief discussion. *ASCD Update 34*(2), 1–8.

Johnson, D., & Johnson, R. (1989) *Leading the cooperative school*. Edina, MN: Interaction Book Company.

LaRocque, L., & Downie, R. (1993) Staff collaboration. *Educators' Notebook 4*(4).

Low, K. (1993). *Designing schools for the 21st century—Critical assessment #4*. Calgary Board of Education 10th Annual Summer Institute for Administrative Teams, Calgary, AB.

Rosenholz, S. (1989). *Teachers' workplace: The social organization of schools*. New York: Longman.

Sarason, S. (1986). And what is the public interest? *American Psychologist, 41*(8), 899-905.

Sarason, S. (1990). *The predictable failure of educational reform*. San Francisco: Jossey-Bass.

Schlecty, P. (1990). *Schools for the 21st century*. San Francisco: Jossey-Bass Inc.

Senge, P. (1994). *The fifth discipline: The art and practice of the learning organization*. New York: Doubleday.

Sergiovanni, T. (1984, February). Leadership and excellence in schooling. *Educational Leadership, 41*(5), 4–13.

Sergiovanni, T. (1992). Moral leadership: Getting to the heart of school improvement. San Francisco: Jossey-Bass.

Sizer, T. (1984). *Horace's compromise: The dilemma of the American high school*. Boston: Houghton Mifflin.

# SUGGESTED READINGS

T. SERGIOVANNI, in a book titled *Leadership for the Schoolhouse: How is it Different? Why is it Important?* (San Francisco: Jossey-Bass, 1996) argues that schools are unique places, requiring their own theories and practices. Readers should find Chapters 3, 4, and 6 interesting as he explores concepts for understanding and building community in schools. Chapters 1, 5, and 10 discuss the kinds of leadership necessary to "deinstitutionalize" change through the politics of virtue, that emphasizes a commitment to the common good; conditions essential for schools as communities to flourish.

WILLIAM PURKEY and JOHN NOVAK (1996) have a very useful book on invitational education titled, *Inviting School Success: A Self-concept Approach to Teaching, Learning, and Democratic Practice*. Chapter 1 explains how invitational education serves as a vehicle for understanding the influence of people, places, policies, programs, and procedures on students. The whole text enriches our discussion of inviting schools, but Chapters 7 and 8 provide particularly practical ideas. The two models for next century schools in Chapter 7 and the systematic process for embodying invitational education in Chapter 8 are especially recommended.

Creating inviting schools and embracing the kinds of change proposed by this book requires changing the culture of schools. MARTIN L. MAEHR and CAROL MIDGLEY (1996) discuss the changing of school culture to bring about a school effectiveness that embraces student motivation and learning. *Transforming School Cultures,* written in collaboration with the Elementary and Middle School Coalitions, examines school cultures, explores the changing of school cultures, and reports on a research effort. Their results show that school change cannot occur without the extensive participation of all concerned, or without committed leadership.

# INDEX